T0163387

The Way of Nothing

Nothing in the Way

The Way of Nothing

Nothing in the Way

Paramananda Ishaya

MANTRA
BOOKS

Winchester, UK
Washington, USA

First published by Mantra Books, 2014
Mantra Books is an imprint of John Hunt Publishing Ltd., Laurel House, Station Approach,
Alresford, Hants, SO24 9JH, UK
office1@jhpbooks.net
www.johnhuntpublishing.com
www.mantra-books.net

For distributor details and how to order please visit the 'Ordering' section on our website.

Text copyright: Paramananda Ishaya 2013

ISBN: 978 1 78279 307 6

All rights reserved. Except for brief quotations in critical articles or reviews, no part of this
book may be reproduced in any manner without prior written permission from the publishers.

The rights of Paramananda Ishaya as author have been asserted in accordance with the
Copyright, Designs and Patents Act 1988.

A CIP catalogue record for this book is available from the British Library.

Design: Lee Nash

Printed and bound by CPI Group (UK) Ltd, Croydon, CR0 4YY

We operate a distinctive and ethical publishing philosophy in all
areas of our business, from our global network of authors to
production and worldwide distribution.

CONTENTS

No One Will Ever Read This

Today I was walking with my girlfriend Shanti, thinking about titles for this book. Then I envisioned myself as a seeker looking for enlightenment in a bookstore; I had been one myself a million times before at the local New Age bookstore in Calgary, Alberta.

In my mind I came to the non-dual section and picked up this book, *No One Will Ever Read This*. I started laughing and said to Shanti, "That is the best title ever! Get it? It's true—no one will ever actually read this because there is no one." She just rolled her eyes and looked at me with an unimpressed "whatever" expression. I admit I was being a little annoying as I threw out idea after idea.

Long before my imaginary visit to the bookstore, I had written the title *The Way of Nothing: Nothing in the Way*. It had just popped into my head. "Eureka!" I thought as I pondered its cleverness. Shanti liked it right away, but that didn't stop me from trying to come up with a better one.

The more I began to think about *The Way of Nothing: Nothing in the Way*, the more it began to reveal its powerful significance— so quickly, in fact, that once I started writing I could not stop. My first book, *A Path of Joy: Popping into Freedom*, was the result of years of inspiration. Writing on the subject of nothing was a totally different experience.

It was as if the energy revealed itself through this new medium of me and my fingers. Perhaps it came more easily because I had the experience of writing the first book. I was so happy about completing *A Path of Joy: Popping into Freedom* that I had no intention of writing anything else. I was looking forward to a break. I felt complete at last and felt I could just relax. That feeling didn't last very long.

As I wrote *The Way of Nothing: Nothing in the Way*, the energy of writing made it even more effortless than before and highly enjoyable. After having some fun trying to come up with a clever, catchy title, it became very clear that the energy had already decided it for me. Who was I to argue with energy?

And who was I writing it for anyway? Who was my audience? After all, a book about nothing, written to no one, and with a lot of nothing to say was going to appeal to exactly no one and sell nothing. How many people really want to read about nothing?

In a very real sense, I had no audience and was writing for no reason at all. The energy meant I was writing for the sheer enjoyment of it. This is the lesson I take from the book: the creative energy that moves and stirs within us is a dance that effortlessly guides us with or without our awareness.

There is a powerful wisdom in nothing at all. This is not only hysterically funny but also very practical in daily life. For this reason, this little book was enjoyable and wonderful to write. Writing was an effortless and blissful task because I had no personal agenda, as I knew that "no one will ever read this."

Beyond being just a clever statement, it's also very true. I did not write this, and nobody is reading this. Despite all beliefs or apparent evidence to the contrary, this is a fact! All books have no authors and no readers. But this is not new information; I read about this very concept in a book before.

And nothing that I could possibly write about is really an original idea. It has all been said before in similar words. All I can do is add a different twist or flavour. All we have are new creative expressions of what has already been said for thousands of years. Who gets the original credit? The same can be said of music: all the music was created a long time ago, and everything "created" since is just a remix of that original creation.

So why write a book about nothing that no one will ever read? I write only out of and for the sake of aliveness. All creative endeavours are alive. In itself, every moment is a creative and wonderful masterpiece happening for no one specifically.

They say that all great expressions emerge from the absence of a "separate creator." In the silence, suddenly and spontaneously the idea for the invention comes up. We call the vehicle for the invention "the inventor," but the inventor is just the puppet through which the energy of invention is expressed.

This is true not just for what we consider great expressions, but for any expression. But what is it that qualifies as a great expression? Is that not subjective? Wouldn't it be something that moves us into a revelation?

Regardless of the medium, that which moves into revelation is a great expression as far as I am concerned. Whether the medium is Starbucks or the Sistine Chapel is irrelevant. I am not attempting to recreate a great expression but trying to unveil the source of *all* expression. This is the attempt. Let's see what happens.

Before beginning to unravel this mystery, I would like to say that everything is the *great* expression of nothingness. This means that even looking for your keys when you are late for work is the greatest of divine masterpieces.

Perception of what makes something miraculous is the reason you don't end up on the front page of the newspaper when you stumble into the bathroom in the middle of the night without stubbing your toe. Such events are not seen as miraculous because people perceive them as ordinary.

Imagine an artist as she paints a beautiful picture of an image she has in her mind of a lake surrounded by mountains. Perhaps at the same time, someone else is creating a different picture of a busy intersection in Hong Kong. We will call these creations art, perhaps, but what is the difference between art and what is happening now?

What we call art is very subjective. This is true of the work of writing as well. One person's beautiful creation is another's disaster.

Every moment everything is happening on a canvas of life. This is scientific fact. Life is being painted with particles such as the atoms and electrons, and with cells, neurons, and endless other distinct yet interconnected pieces that come together like the colours of the spectrum. They are complete within black and white or nothingness and everything-ness.

When we understand this, we see that the girl painting the painting *is* the painting. *She* is the masterpiece, along with the chair she sits on in the room and the image in her head as she paints. As you read this, you are not a person who is reading but a part of the scene or masterpiece that is happening now. In this scene *you* are a work of art, a display of wonder happening right now.

I would congratulate you on your masterpiece, but how would you react? If I went up to you and started clapping, saying, "You did it—look at you! How wonderful! Good job! Bravo!" would you not think I was a complete idiot? This is not different from enlightenment, liberation, and freedom.

A sage does not *do* anything to be a masterpiece but simply sees it. This seeing is freedom! If there is any point at all, it is to see the masterpiece that remains hidden when you think of yourself as separate from the total scene. When you see this scene, you become everything, and even the separate individual that you believe you are becomes part of the background of colours, shapes, and textures. Forget what that looks like! Trying to figure it out is a waste of time. Just keep having fun painting.

Are you seeing the picture that is being painted? The agenda is not so much to paint you a picture but to help you dismantle it. Nothing is the agenda.

But what do I know? I am not an artist.

All about Nothing

I truly attained nothing from complete, unexcelled Enlightenment.
—Buddha

It seems strange that there can be any information about nothing. After all, the very word means the absence of anything at all. What can you say or write about the absence of anything? Discussing it would seem to destroy nothing by making it something again. Yet instead of saying nothing or having no writing on these pages, we are going to use one concept to destroy all the other concepts.

If it helps, visualise all these pages as blank as you read them; this will remind you that there is a greater teaching behind these words appearing. This is what is meant by no teaching, no student, no teacher. We are not ignoring them but pointing to nothingness, which dissolves the teacher, student, and teaching.

Reportedly, Ramana Maharishi sat in silence for many years while people came to visit him on Arunachala Mountain. Later on he said that his teaching was the silence. If that did not do the trick for a student, he would say, "All there is, is consciousness." If the student was still puzzled, he would start gabbing away about this and that. Many books have been written about Ramana Maharishi, who taught silence or nothingness as the ultimate teaching. He himself never wrote a book.

Anything we can think of automatically negates what the word "nothing" represents. In other words, the pointer is not the point, the object is not the subject, and the thing is not the no-thing. What we are attempting to describe here *is* the point, which remains obvious even while it seems elusive because of our own habit of thinking too much. Make no mistake—nothing is a funny subject that probably is best understood through laughter.

Regardless of how this silence is explored in this material or in others, there is a resonance beyond the concepts presented. The role that oneness plays is to chip away at the subtleties of conceptualisation to the heart of it all. Liberation happens through resonance or a readiness that no one can force. I liken it to a kind of maturity or ripeness in the seeker. By seeker, I am referring to someone seeking God, enlightenment, freedom, peace, joy, or harmony.

Even after liberation, this receptivity to oneness remains, but not as something to understand or figure out. The nothingness itself is seen in everything because it *is* the subject of everything.

It is impossible to describe what nothing is, yet words and ideas such as those presented here come out of this nothingness as if it is attempting to describe itself. What the word represents is *all that is*. At the same time, what the word points to is obvious and does not need explanation. So what is the point in repeating concepts about nothing at all?

The point is to point to the place of no point and no journey to nowhere or what is called nothing. It is a hopeless quest for the separate individual (you), yet beyond the words and labels is what is. My hope is to demonstrate that this hopeless quest for you is the cover story for what is actually aliveness and wonder beyond imagination.

This authority of nothingness stands on its own and reveals what is without reason or purpose but simply for the love of what it is. This is a paradox for the mind of an individual who seeks to know and understand that which is always just out of reach. In fact, it is hopeless because the you that you think you are never actually gets there. You may discover this good news sooner than you think. In truth, it is always there before you think about it anyway.

When we refer to the self and our true nature as eternal,

infinite, magnificent, and divine (fill in your own big words), we create a sense that the hugeness of what we are is beyond our ability to achieve. You may ask, "How can little ol' me with all my problems find that bigness within?" While we may *be* this infinite bigness, our seeking of it as an object can put us in an impossible position. When you seek the divine, something is always missing. We can undertake a tiresome and often painful spiritual quest leading to extreme highs and lows. Welcome to duality!

This bipolar quality is very common in the quest. Seekers will sometimes take extreme measures to get the peace they want. This thirst for peace is understandable because it is well worth it. Anyone who has tasted the sublime peace of silence knows that it is undeniably delicious. It becomes an addiction, however, when we misunderstand the origin of peace. Peace is assumed to be an object just like the divine. It is the drug of choice for the spiritual addict. Give me some of that bliss to stop the suffering and craving!

What makes the quest worse is that the glimpses of the divine coming though meditation, contemplation, or just dumb luck torture us after we've experienced them. "How can I stay in that peace and stillness?" we might ask. "Perhaps I will try harder to let go!"

This craziness can end in freedom, especially under the guidance of a teacher, but there are no guarantees. But you do not need to become a "bipolar bear." For some, an understanding of what is true is enough for liberation to occur, but it is not my place to predict what may or may not happen. I only aim to keep coming back to nothing at all so that we can see what happens.

You would think that the more effort we put toward achieving our highest desire (such as enlightenment), the happier we would be. But often the reverse is true. We never get there because what we are seeking is an object or notion in our heads. Some of us treasure these notions more than anything, which can make the path to freedom seem insurmountable. Getting fed up with our notions can also lead to freedom, but again there is no way to be sure if this will work.

The reason this quest for enlightenment is hopeless is that *you cannot be an accurate gauge or guide to your own freedom!* This is probably the most important concept in the book. In other words, you cannot do it yourself. If it does happen, it will happen without you! If you think you are going to get any special secrets from me, sorry, I don't have any. All I can do is entice you to see that you are already free. Is this a paradox? Yes and no.

Listen; what you think of as you is not capable of attaining anything. This you is not the subject but an imposter pretending to be the subject. What you think you are is really an object. You are a lovely, sexy object, I agree, but still an object. In the pure subjectivity of the infinite, an object can only come and go or not come at all. Liberation comes from seeing this you as an object. Seeing this is understanding that you never have left what is or what you truly are. This is the non-duality of the real *you*.

The spiritual quest can be painful because of a simple misunderstanding. Conceptualising our true nature and seeking out this concept as a goal is painful. Obviously, our nature itself is unmoved and untouched by this dilemma, which can be solved by simple clarity. Clarity happens naturally during the exploration of the divine. As we approach the space of no-mind without concepts and without you, we begin to discern the real from the false. This discernment can take decades, years, or an instant, but the sole purpose of talking about nothingness, if there is one, is to provide a soil in which easiness and simplicity flourish so we can see the infinite as it is. You and I have no control over how long the process takes because there is no separate you or I. There is only the mystery of nothingness, some laughter, and hopefully a lot of "I don't know." The more you don't know, the better.

Ask yourself: "What am I?" If you say, "I am infinite or free or

God," is that not just a concept? Of course if you think you are nothing, that is also a concept. No matter what you come up with, anything you can know about yourself is only another idea. The only real and honest answer the mind can come up with is, "I don't know." Even if I am talking to an enlightened sage, you still do not know what you are because it is beyond ideas and concepts. It is unknown, unborn, and alive. It is the knowingness without someone there to know. You can speak with authority and say, "I am this," or "it is this" but that is coming out of nothingness, without you there to claim anything specific as belonging to you.

The concept of nothing is the closest I can come to describing the nature of self. I chose it on purpose because it is not a foundation for more concepts. It is designed to dissolve, leaving only what is alive underneath the labels. This nothingness is concept-free and ultimately it is everything you seek, no matter what the form is. It is the highest joy, the highest attainment you seek through spiritual or material means. It is the secret treasure that is *all that is here in this reality.* Only the fascination with anything else seems to obscure it.

The beautiful thing is that if you are willing to give this still, silent nothingness a chance, you will get everything your heart desires and more. This process will not look like you want it to, but it will be greater than you can imagine. The aliveness of what is, is self-sufficient and needs nothing added to it. The hard truth is that life works much better without you. All you can do is get in the way, and indeed this is all that ever seems to happen. This is the cosmic joke, which is not very funny, at least until you disappear into nothingness and laugh for no reason at all—that is the divine comedy.

Liberation is not an attainment but the simple abiding in the unborn and eternal nature of your essence. In this essence you are infinitely bigger than you can imagine yet also much smaller, so small, in fact, that you might dissolve. Without you there,

there is the discovery of what is left. This step is natural and effortless, as you will see, and no amount of thought will bring you there. I'm not saying don't think about it, even though that would be wasting time. We can meditate and use our favourite tools and techniques, but what happens is in the hands of God, Buddha, or Baby Jesus (in other words, nobody's hands).

The magic is that often when things don't go the way we want them to and we are completely frustrated, our grip on identity will loosen. However you look at it, the result is inevitable because everything happening now is happening *in* and *as* nothingness.

Good luck with the discovery!

Nothing but Freedom

When talking about freedom, we immediately must refer to its opposite: limitation and bondage. Freedom is something we don't feel we have; maybe other people have it, but we don't. Of course the alternative idea that we are free already does not change much about how we experience our lives day to day except that we might have a nice thought floating by once in a while.

I am embarrassed to say that I was one of those people walking around thinking that I was enlightened and superior to almost everyone. Then I would flip back into the insecurity and anxiety of the bipolar bear. Living in this duality is not a fun way to approach what is, and thankfully it is not true anyway. The label of nothing is great because this nothingness is even closer than our breath. Where there is nothing at all, there is freedom. This is how close to freedom everyone is. Often you will hear teachers say that you are already free. This is a nice idea, isn't it?

The idea of you being free comes with a bit of confusion. Firstly, freedom could imply that there is a you that is already free or a you that will one day be free. Both of these concepts are not true. (It is useful to remember that all concepts, including this one, are not true.)

The nature of nothingness is that there is nothing at all. This is already all that is. It is because of this that you can say that you are already free. However, in the experience (for a lack of a better word) of nothingness, a separate you is not there to be free or not. Being free or separate is another notion floating in nothingness. The separate self does not like this idea of not being there because it is not included as the one that is free.

The only thing the separate you can do is continue to think it's going to achieve something. This is the separate seeker. Do not worry about it; simply allow it to do what it is designed to do—seek.

Fear can arise when the thought of nothing comes up. Let me reassure the separate you (if you still think you have one), for whatever it's worth, that the thought of nothing is not nothingness itself. Nothingness itself does not have a thought of nothing in the purest sense. You do not know what nothingness is or feels like because it is beyond the ability of the intellect to know or understand.

Whatever you think you can know about nothingness results from a memory of experiences, including any feelings such as peace or joy. Often people who believe they are spiritual will say, "Oh, I know what that is." If you say "I know" a lot, chances are you don't know what you're talking about but you have a good grasp of your experiences. Grasping onto experiences is what the separate individual does. To grasp at knowledge is actually grasping at dead knowledge, not wisdom. True wisdom does not know anything.

Maybe this nothingness is actually quite lovely and delicious. Maybe it is the absolute bliss of God. Maybe it is the light of Heaven. After all, it is your true nature. Whatever you may think about your true nature, it is always greater than you can conceive yet simpler than you can imagine. I don't make up the rules! So whenever you think you are grasping the infinite, remember it is greater than you think, and let it reveal itself without the "little grasper." What is left when there is no grasper? You now have no reason to think about it anymore. The grasping and the grasper are both happening in nothingness. There is no need to change the purpose of grasping—it is what it is.

It would be too simple to say that your identity as separate is just a thought since there are many so-called signs of limitation or of being separate. However, you could say that all the signs of separation are just thoughts or objects appearing in and out of nothing and nowhere.

Some of these signs of separation are having an energetic

feeling in the body (such as in the heart), thinking you are the thinker of your thoughts, and believing that you are in control of what happens. All of these signs of separation are apparent, but trying to convince someone of this is extremely challenging, not to mention a waste of time. What is magical, however, is that a readiness or receptivity can occur in which the person sees through the notion of separateness. This is a miracle of grace. Suddenly, without you there, the truth appears. Pointers in life such as the one you are reading can somehow cross space and time, and *bam*—there it is.

It makes sense that individuals believe in their individuality because that is how we are designed and programmed. We are not going to get into why we are programmed as such because that is also a waste of time, and more importantly, I have no idea why. I have some theories (no reason at all, or nothingness is bored), but I still don't know why, and I don't care.

It is more useful to look at how we are programmed to identify ourselves as separate individuals so that we may take a step backwards so to speak. Starting over with a blank slate is always a useful approach to becoming free. This is the Zen of emptying the cup or pushing the reset button to clear the programming. The nature of nothingness is to be empty. To start by emptying our heads of concepts is a great way to begin. Apart from not taking things seriously, it is the only rule. Emptying is the way to joy, contentment, and wisdom.

Right now you can perhaps sense that you are here. This can be called a sense of self or a sense that you exist. When you are not thinking or identifying with any object in particular, there can be this awareness or consciousness without anything else. This awareness happens whenever you are not thinking. When you wake up from deep sleep, this consciousness comes without any identifying. It is like a brand new empty car before someone opens the door, jumps in, turns the key, drives to God knows where, and then crashes (sorry, I am getting off track—too much coffee today).

This awareness is just empty consciousness or the fancy, enlightened-sounding "pure consciousness." But then this consciousness seems to spontaneously identify with the body, energy, and thoughts, and then the personal identity is formed around the object of the body. Consciousness identifies itself as a you by accident or coincidence. The only other option it has is to identify with nothingness, but that has not been presented as a valuable option. This is the divine joke, since it is already the absolute impersonal consciousness.

With the innocence of a child, consciousness makes this simple mistake of identifying. This is why the most common response to waking up is "oops!" or "duh!" It is almost embarrassing that this misidentifying happened. But because it is like a child, we don't punish this consciousness but laugh at the innocent mistake it made. Laughter and bliss are the appropriate responses to enlightenment because it is all a joke, as silly as the simple childlike belief that monsters are in the closet.

Through consciousness, everything seems to appear and happen to an individual. We are all like puppets running around taking everything personally except for the moments when we forget to think and fall back into nothingness. So where did the pure consciousness come from?

The sense of self that appears *in* and *as* consciousness that is identified with something comes from nothingness. The ability to even be aware happens in nothingness. Why this happens is a mystery to me, but what is fascinating is that the totality of every single event comes out of nothingness. This nothing that we label "blank, empty, and ordinary" contains the entire manifestations of the densest to the subtlest objects we can perceive.

We have known about the nature of nothing for thousands and perhaps tens of thousands of years. It has been written about in the Vedas, which scientists are starting to find are much older than they had presumed.

All of our senses function because of the absolute. The absolute nothingness does all of the perceiving through the senses, and we just take ownership of this process. We literally steal the natural process and try to control it. That there appears to be an individual responsible for the perceiving is just a coincidence and an anomaly. Our very own personal sense of self arises and subsides in this nothingness. We take it seriously because we believe it is the subject or centre of the world. But would you take it seriously if you saw this "you-centre" as a tiny dot in an infinite sea?

This nothingness is both ordinary and extraordinary at the same time, and this makes it spectacular. It makes our journey to achieve freedom and then realise we are already free awesome.

Nothing in Your Way

As individuals who are seeking freedom, peace, and the highest good, how can we achieve our highest desires?

The truth is, there is no great achievement in life other than seeing the absence of someone achieving. Everything happening right now is a great achievement for no one.

Getting up in the middle of the night and stumbling over to the washroom without stubbing your toe is the same as coming up with a breakthrough mathematical theory. Both events are spontaneous and only through the eyes of the individual is one better than another. All events happening now are the same— equivalent miracles of nothingness.

Srinivasa Ramanujan was a famous mathematician from India. He is not as famous for his actual formulas as he is for how they arrived to him. Frustrating his colleges, his process was one of intuition; the formulas just came to him out of nowhere. These formulas are now the basis for theories in physics. He skipped the mental process or "proofs" needed and went straight to the end result. For decades mathematicians have been working on these formulas and filling in the blanks for theories about various phenomena such as black holes.

Whether you arrive at the answer in an instant or dedicate your life to mental processes, the result is the same. It all happens spontaneously without a separate analyser. The thinking and analysing happen simultaneously with the nothingness, and this process is also spontaneous.

Only through thinking can we distinguish and categorise achievements in terms of degrees of specialness. Discovering where you left your key is no different from discovering a historically relevant theory. When we die, most of us don't get awards for special achievement (maybe one for best dressed, I don't know).

Through recognising that nothing is in the way, our highest good is revealed. All the obstacles are removed because they were never there. Enlightenment occurs without you there to achieve it. Only active conceptualising masks what is already the unattainable highest bliss. By moving in the exact opposite direction and not thinking, it becomes possible to provide the necessary elements for awakening to happen. Unfortunately for the individual, there are no guarantees of liberation or standard time frames in which it will take place.

It feels completely unfair when we recognise that even with all the "correct" understanding and right tools for the job, we are not guaranteed liberation. The only thing that comes close to guaranteeing us this is guidance from a teacher, and this is assuming that the teacher is actually free. Whatever the external path this teacher may represent is irrelevant if liberation has happened; the resonance of silence or truth is sufficient to dissolve separation. This silence is a spontaneous gift from nothingness to open us up to the way of nothing. The teacher's only job is to point out that you are in the way and that ultimately there is nothing in the way!

The harder we try to let go, the more we are in the way. This is not always bad, however, because sometimes we need to do things over and over until we see the futility of them. At any moment, the identity can lose interest in itself, just like a child being distracted with a toy. The effort of trying, as well as paying attention to the same old stories in our heads, gets old. Seeing that we do this is half the battle.

On one hand, you could view individuals who are trying hard to be free as "doing it wrong" because they should be allowing it all. On the other, they might quickly understand that their efforts are in vain and then liberation could happen. Often a spiritual release happens when we are the most frustrated and tired of trying, so keep it up! You can figure it out! (Not really.)

Individuals who start off doing the right thing by surrendering and letting go might never wake up. There is no formula that works other than allowing the direct experience of nothingness. Actually, nothingness is all that can happen during the process of liberation. How liberation looks is part of the surprise for each explorer. Despite how it looks, despite the path, and despite experiences, it is only about nothing at all. There are no special liberated beings. Buddha, Jesus, and Bob all recognised that all there is, is no one. When there is no one, then all that exists is unity! Unity is the spectacular and extraordinary expansion of infinite consciousness, which is simple, ordinary nothingness and everything-ness in one vast soup of absolutely nothing.

A genuine desire to "know thyself" is sufficient to realise your true nature. A willingness to do what it takes with a spirit of openness is useful. But there are no rules; nothing is required. In the end, the only thing standing in your way is you, and this you is only an idea that has been caressed with attention to give it the appearance of subjective reality. This you is actually a part of objective reality.

The greatest hidden desire in the individual is for nothing since it is the foundation of contentment. To be complete and satisfied is the natural way of being. Fullness comes from not having to feed the identity's desires; doing so is only being in your own way. These desires are only masked as end results leading to future joy. They are attached to the separate individual.

In liberation, desires appear in nothing and return to nothing. Surrendering becomes automatic when we understand that remaining content with nothing is more enjoyable than chasing after objects that only lead to empty hunger and cravings. Something is always missing in this vicious cycle of wanting.

We can have our cake and eat it too by seeing that nothing is in the way and that the identity is only another movement within consciousness that comes and goes. Sometimes it desires this and sometimes that. When there is nothing in the way, there is no longer a need or addiction to satisfy the identity's selfish desires. Don't feed the monster!

Allowing Silence becomes a simple, open welcoming of what will come. The result is a spontaneous fulfilment in which we don't focus narrowly on objects but see the whole universe as the source of abundance. In other words, after seeing this, we can do what we want.

This is not laziness but putting the horse before the cart. With the source of joy, it does not matter what we get or don't get. We are truly free to have it all. To chase after the things such as money or relationships without an ulterior motive is to truly play like a child. Whatever you want to do or have, go for it! (What would Jesus do?)

Nothing is forbidden, and everything is an invitation to play. Through allowing nothingness we can see over and over again without judgement if we still appear to be in the way. This is an eternal invitation to see. Of course we can still have a concept that living in nothing means anarchy and is an excuse for the mind to do what it wants. This is only dangerous to the individual in separation who believes in concepts, but to nothingness, there is always a spontaneous flow of goodness that makes all apparent choices okay. This is not a concept or a way to live—it is simply nothing allowing everything. But if putting your hand in the fire hurts, may I suggest that you stop doing it! Duh!

Have you seen the cosmic joke? Do you understand that there has never been anything in the way of your bliss? Imagine the joy in discovering that you have had the ultimate treasure in your heart the whole time, staring at you for eternity. How hard would you laugh, knowing that all your efforts to see this treasure were only to make liberated beings, angels, and all the gods laugh. Believe me, they are already laughing at you. Why not join in with them? You are hysterically funny.

As long as we appear to be in the way of nothing, we take things seriously. How funny is that? How can you be in the way of nothingness itself? That is the joke. There is nothing to take seriously, especially nothingness, which never takes things seriously. This is why it is called no-thing. Think about it!

You

We can put the term "nothing" in the right context by saying that nothing is the experience of being all there is without a separate entity that experiences it. This experience of nothing is illuminating and wonderful. There is nothing sad, dull, or boring about being in nothingness. On the contrary, it is full of life without any qualities whatsoever, which is what makes its normality surprisingly fantastic.

If you can begin to see nothing in the "right" frame of mind, then when I say, "You are nothing," you will get excited and perhaps start jumping around the room shouting, "Yes! Yes! Yes!" However, I would not recommend going around telling people you are nothing—let's keep that secret between us, okay?

One of my favourite sages, Nisargadatta Maharaj, has been quoted as saying, "Wisdom is Knowing I am Nothing, Love is Knowing I am Everything." Through exploring this nothingness, the conclusion that we are nothing becomes free of conceptualisation. In fact, it is not that we are nothing but that there is only nothingness at the heart of freedom. Of course you can choose whatever idea you wish to represent nothingness.

The concept of what being nothing would seem like to you or your mind gets crushed under the non-conceptual reality of what being without you actually *is*. This is the wisdom of nothing in which only the highest good can come.

Events don't always look as if they are for the highest good, especially for the separate individual. If you consider that the point of being is to *wake up* or *be enlightened*, then all events are a sacred invitation to this rediscovery. Everything becomes a constant call to liberation.

How we understand this concept that you are nothing is completely backwards in society and more importantly in spirituality. It is indeed an insult to say that you are nothing even though it is the highest compliment anyone has ever bestowed upon an individual. By saying, "You are nothing," I am saying you are the absolute infinite. I am saying that you are the greatest! Again, please do not say that to your neighbour, or you might get punched in the face!

Even science does not like finding nothing. Scientists keep searching for the ultimate something by smashing apart particles. That nothingness is the answer behind what science is looking for is the great cosmic joke. The scientist herself is nothing searching for nothing. I mean that as a compliment.

The scientist is already the totality of everything she could ever hope to achieve in terms of finding an answer. She is the infinite itself. Nothingness hides that fact as the final truth. Of course the gas station attendant has that same revelation waiting for him as the guru, the billionaire, and even the lawyer. Knowing this is humbling for the intellectuals of the world. This is where being a little slow like me has its advantages.

We all take part in a comedy of achievement. We achieve nothing, figuratively and literally. This truth can lead to a sort of depression if we have not seen the concept of nothing we hold in our minds in its entirety. The concept itself has more of an attraction than the direct experiencing of nothing.

It is not a nice thing to realise that you are not special. It does have some advantages, however, such as the relief of not having to feed your self-image. Traditionally, getting stuck in this place of seeing you are nothing but not letting go enough for the total bliss of enlightenment to happen is called being in the desert. Sounds scary, doesn't it? This desert is a hopeless place in which the last bits of sad, poor me, who thinks, "I am just a plain old nothing," wander around. Where is the love? Joy? Bliss? Contentment?

Being in the desert is only temporary and might not even happen necessarily. If it does happen, it can take years or even lifetimes to get past. Having a teacher point out what you cannot see can help lessen the time spent in the desert. The mind can become very subtle at this point, and perhaps it can become mentally enlightened.

In one instant, you will laugh at how seriously you took yourself and then the desert will disappear, and there is only the fullness of love—all thanks to nothing. Amen and hallelujah! Once you have seen it through or when liberation of no one special happens, it is exhilarating to say the least. It gives you an unbounded freedom to play without any limits.

You might think that freedom looks like giving up your job and moving into a cave, but more than likely everything on the outside will look exactly the same. The only difference will be that you will no longer feel the pressure and responsibility of being weighed down by a serious you. The concept of you is no more.

What does the concept of "no-you" or being free look like? Let go of the idea of no-you. I used to check in to see if I was there or not. This is pointless and brings up the question: Who would want to be doing that anyway? The separate individual may still appear after waking up, but it appears as a concept to the nothingness you are. The you comes and goes, but you no longer need to concern yourself with it because you have lost interest in it. The interest is in staying in the divine nothingness, which does not care about such things as, "Do I have an ego?" or "Am I really enlightened?" Both concepts can come and go.

So what is being enlightened? Ironically, it can look like "being more you." How is this even possible when you are nothing? Is this not a paradox? Perhaps it is when we think about it, but by being nothingness the separate you dissolves and frees you to be, to play, and to enjoy your life. This "new" you can do exactly what it has always done before and maybe even with greater ease.

When the you drops away, so does the friction of life. You fill up whatever role you desire. If you are a banker, you are nothingness pretending to be a banker. If you throw away your clothes for robes and become a teacher, then you are nothingness pretending to be a teacher.

When you step out of the way, the essence that is unique to you shines in its glory—like my radiant, divine sexiness, for example.

No-You

One of the most fascinating discoveries is that there is no you. There is no you as you think you are. You come and go as part of a story.

Maybe it is not so easy to see that there is no you, but you can easily find out that you are not what you think you are. Finding out what you are not is a great game with huge benefits.

Just because we think a certain way does not make something real. A perception is not truth, and perceptions can change with new information. What is true does not change and is eternal because it simply *is*. Truth does not *represent* something, it *is*. Perception represents a view, position, or idea. Perception is a way of seeing but not the actual seeing itself. We can clear the mirror of perception so that it closely resembles truth, but this is only clarity, not truth.

There is a very simple question we can ask: What is real and what is not? We find the answer by exploring the real, which comes about through shedding light on yourself.

Forget about which self you are looking at—with gentle curiosity, just play with what is the truth about what is happening or not happening now. When it stops being about thinking and starts being about seeing, it gets easier.

The you that appears in the world is taken for granted as being as real and as solid as a rock. Nothing can be further from the truth. This you is entirely fragile and vulnerable. You are susceptible to the power of nothingness, which gobbles you up without any warning at all. This is a wonderful mystery that goes unnoticed because of its familiarity.

In the world, you are seen as the foundation and centre of everything important. You are the centre of the universe, but not because you want it that way; it is simply in the nature of identification as a separate person. This centre includes the you that will one day wake up, be free, or be enlightened. Everything seems to revolve around this you. All your choices, actions, and even the results affect you and everything this you claims to own.

Underneath the you that demands attention is a quiet selflessness that does not have any special point of reference at all. In it, you are already free from yourself. Maybe you don't want all this attention on you because it is unbearable to be so important and special. It can be frustrating when such attention keeps returning to you like an endless yo-yo or "you-you." You are literally the star of your own show, and nobody can convince you otherwise.

We can try to shake this identity loose, but this is like trying not to hear a loud noise. All we can do is cover it up or think of something pleasant to lessen the disturbance. We can only muffle the sound. As soon as we take our hands from our ears, there the noise is again.

You have no control over whether the noise of you is there or being silenced. You can, however, see through its noise to the source of silence, which makes the arising and subsiding of the you-centre irrelevant.

You are a tricky subject when analysed. Even through the eye of non-duality, you can easily become a paradox. However, this trickiness is apparent only, and hopefully you have a clear under-standing of the simplicity of it all as we proceed in the mystery of no-you.

Whether you are here or not is not up to you. You don't have to do anything but allow. Don't worry, it will all become clear to you or no-you—or maybe not. None of this material has anything to do with you. It is all about nothingness. If you are conf-you-sed, that is good. The only advice I can give to you is don't take it seriously.

When you can come to the point when you can laugh at yourself, you are close to freedom. When you think you are close to freedom, laugh at yourself even harder because this is ridiculous! This you will never be free! Relax and enjoy the show as it seems to unfold either for you or maybe not for you. Maybe the show unfolds despite you. Maybe you are the show.

Despite what we may hear or read about freedom not being about you, there still remains an underlying assumption that it happens to you. This is totally okay as part of the story and could not be any other way. The you-centre is happening in a sea of nothingness and nowhere. It is a dot or a tiny shell in this sea, a suggestion. It is suggested to no one (or consciousness) that there is an individual. This is the divine hypnosis and the beginning of the illusion of a path to somewhere. This somewhere does not exist. In the way of nothing, the path is more accurately labelled a path to nowhere.

When talking about there being a "no-you-centre," we refer to the complete freedom of being identified with you as a separate event. This you is an event, yes, but not separate. The big you without a centre is eventless. There is nothing wrong with this you-event, and nothing could be done to change anything about it anyway. With readiness it is seen for what it is.

Only an appearance of you (as a centre) could change. This is why how you think of yourself changes. Your self-image changes over time and is not the same as it was when you were a child. This is clear evidence that this separate you is an object that seems to change with time.

This is what we call going bananas. Every single one of us is going totally bananas! The fact that people actually believe they have got themselves "together" is quite hilarious. If anything, falling apart is closer to sanity, but what do I know? I am not a psychologist, just a patient.

Putting an idea or image together over the span of a hundred years is what we call life. Where are all these images going? Self-image is a perception that ends when the movie is over. When you remove image from self-image, you get self. Self has no image. The self only pretends to go bananas.

If you become a better meditator, it is this "you-image" that is a better meditator. If you think you are more awake than before or you are closer to freedom, then this represents an appearance of you in the story. Again this is perfectly natural in the story. Don't let this frustrate you; you can't help moving toward freedom since the you-centre has no choice at all. Just for fun, try to stop moving. That is you trying to stop, which is also part of the story.

What is a story? It is a series of events, including the event of a you.

Exploring nothingness is the way, but who is doing that? Is it the event or the eventless? Is it the centre or the centre-less? Is it the concept or the concept-less?

Anything you do or don't do for freedom's sake is the joke because you are doing it, and you are part of the story happening. Even trying to let go and surrender is a part of the story. What are you surrendering to? Who is doing that?

The you-centre says, "Well, if there is no me, then I will just do what I want and I'm free—yippee for me!"

You can't take this seriously. It is all a big laugh. When you notice that you are taking it seriously and thinking too much, feel free to laugh at yourself. You might think losing yourself in the silence or not thinking is a serious task, but it is a joyful dance, I swear.

Welcome to the comedy of you. We should receive a manual about this as children. You are going to both love and hate the comedy of you. You are going to work on your self-image. You are going to fall in love and have your heart broken. You'll get rich and lose it all. Then you are going to look for enlightenment, think you have it, and then lose it again. Okay, this is your body, and these are your parents. Good luck, and remember it has nothing to do with you, so don't take it personally.

You may be wondering how you cannot take things seriously. But the seriousness falls away. Little by little or all at once, it falls away. When it completely falls away, this is freedom. Did you know that about freedom?

Even though seriousness does fall away, there is no guarantee it might not come back. Staying open to what may come is humility and lessens the chance of inner turmoil. Until the arrogance of being in control of life dissolves, the struggle of you continues.

Maybe hearing it over again and again will help, but maybe not. With me and other students, I have seen the effort and trying falling away at a certain point. This means the same as surrendering or letting go of the you-centre.

By letting go of you, you are letting go of all identification and concepts. Of course you don't actually do this. In the way of nothing, and in the silence of no-you, all falseness disappears into the truth. This is an instant by-product of nothingness.

I used to think that letting go was something that you do, but now I see that it just happens by itself. It would look as if I was choosing to stop trying, but the effort stopped by itself after a period of my trying really hard. I got exhausted and then gave up. As I said, I thought I was giving up, but giving up happened without my decision. My decision was only in the story.

Instead of giving you advice to let go and surrender, I could just as easily say to this you-centre to try harder and hold on tighter, as that also seems to be the key to freedom. In the way of nothing, there are no rules to get to nowhere. Actually right now there is nothing in the way.

Don't worry; I am not going to tell you that nowhere is now here because that is a cheesy thing to say that I am absolutely beyond saying. Damn it, I just said it! That just came from nowhere. I will stop now here.

What is meant by freedom and no-you in the first place? Let's look at what no-you really is in essence. First of all, the way of nothing is ordinary and simple. Ultimately, nobody sees that there is only this amazing nothingness. This you that you think you are comes and goes in this nothingness all the time. It is not a solid entity and can and does slip away constantly for everyone, even the unspiritual.

When you get what you want, the you-centre disappears. When you fall in love, you disappear. When you eat a hamburger, drink beer, or eat chocolate, you disappear. There are no guarantees about when you disappear, except for maybe during sleep, laughter, and enlightenment.

When you disappear, you usually don't freak out and scream, "Oh my God, I'm not here. Where am I? Help!" The reason you don't go crazy is that suddenly, if only for a moment, you are content with nothing. You have abandoned everything in favour of the way of nothing. Make no mistake, there is only one way—the way of nothing, and everyone is basking in this nothingness right now. This is the "now here nowhere" that is a path of joy.

The reason you don't freak out in this nothingness is because there is no you to freak out. But this nothingness, which is more natural and ordinary than breathing, is seen as an object of fear. What's hilarious is that we fear what we are already experiencing all the time. Our own concept of what nothingness is frightens us. Since it ultimately means our death, that makes sense, but still there is no way of knowing what death is until it happens. Maybe death is lovely—who knows? Maybe we have death confused with capital-L Life. Wouldn't that be funny! We don't wake up in the morning after a good night's sleep and scream in terror, "Oh my God, I died last night!"

What we call nothingness is irrelevant, but it's important that we are both talking about the same thing. By stripping away all the mumbo-jumbo surrounding nothingness, we can begin to simplify what is already the simplest subject ever. The difficulty results in explaining how ridiculously simple and easy nothingness is. It really is nothing! But get ready to have your mind blown because nothing has a big surprise for you.

What separates enlightenment and ignorance is the belief that you are a separate individual. This belief is also what separates the arrogance of being someone and the humility of being no one. In the way of nothing, humility is all there is. Within humility is the rising and falling away of the arrogance of being a somebody. The humility of nothingness is not something that you can attain, and only by your absence is it revealed.

Even though we all disappear into nothingness many times a day, we don't recognise this as an important event. If there is no you, who or what would think it was important? Who would care to report on it? Disappearing into nothingness isn't really important because it does not need or ask for special attention. Nothingness is too familiar to register as a peak or divine experience. Its ordinariness is what makes the way of nothing so amazing. You will fall in love with its obviousness.

Through the repeated experience of silence, nothingness reveals its true value but normally it does not advertise this to us. This is the advertisement here: try it, you'll like it. Open bliss!

Nothingness is more obvious than slapping yourself in the face. Go ahead and try. Did it work? Are you enlightened yet?

In the mystery of no-you, the self is recognised as a concept-less full nothingness. This is all there is. Enlightenment is seeing the eternity of this unity that, while having nothing to do with you, seems to hold the story of you in a loving embrace. In the humility of enlightenment, the story of you loses interest, and the way of nothing captures all the attention.

What was before seen as a moment of nothing happening or blankness is now revealed to be the greatest hidden treasure in the world. How magnificent and awesome is this God who gave us nothing and everything? What else could you possibly ask for? You literally have everything, as well as nothing at all. How cool is that?

The joke is, we are already free and have everything the you is looking for in nothing at all. There is literally nothing in the way of that ever! This is the universal grace we all look for.

Nothingness is the grace, and it is all there is.

Even though this still nothingness is the most important thing for a seeker to experience, it is not seen as such. The concept of freedom or enlightenment is held in the mind, in place of nothing, as an ideal to chase after and seems preferable to what seems like a boring, dull nothing at first. We see this concept of freedom as more important than the ordinary oneness of nothing. We see freedom as more special and important because it involves a story of you achieving something other than the only thing available—nothing.

Something special makes somebody special, which in turn makes up the story of life. Of course this is completely nuts. In this story, the you-centre cannot have anything except change. Like grabbing a handful of sand and trying to keep it from falling through your fingers, it all slips away into nothing. It always comes back to nothingness.

Don't worry; you are still special because your story is special and unique. I am not trying to patronise you; I really believe that. I am not one to negate the story in favour of the way of nothing. Your story is full of ups and downs, and no one can ever take that away. Also, your story of awakening is unique and has a certain *je ne sais quoi*. But the humility of nothingness is not beyond anything, including your story. Nothingness allows everything because there is nothing but nothingness; it is inclusiveness in the extreme.

I sometimes have this funny idea that after we die we look at the highlights of our lives in a huge stadium filled with angels, as though we were watching a DVD of the bloopers of our lives. I think we would have a big laugh at everything we did for nothing and for no reason at all. Can you see yourself and your story? Would you be laughing or crying?

The story of you will continue even after there is nobody there. You simply won't be in the way of it anymore; you will be in the way of nothing. Your story or dream in this life has a way of working itself out in the most spontaneous, effortless way. If you want your dream to turn into a nightmare, then by all means get involved and take charge of it. This is a guaranteed disaster.

The exploration of no-you is an amazing mystery that I equate with having your cake and eating it too. You get the bliss of not having to negotiate with yourself or others while at the same experiencing the joy of being alive and active in the world. The most practical and intelligent design has already been built into the fabric of life, and it is simple by design. Nothingness is truly wonderful in its practicality. It pays your taxes and washes your dishes while you sit back and laugh.

I remember being depressed having to get up in the morning for work. The thought of facing my world was scary. Even simple tasks like washing the dishes took tremendous energy. I was exhausted. I was self-absorbed and stuck with no light in sight. Somehow I felt that there was a way, but I had no idea what that way was. How would I get rid of me?

Now doing the dishes is a sacred act of Zen, and getting up is not such a big deal. You disappear in the Zen moment, and you kill the Buddha, becoming the Zen of nothing. Then the dishes seem to wash themselves. The bliss of nothing washes them. Nothingness is the highest bliss, and it is in everything, including taking out the trash.

Before I continue, I need to tell you something very important. Please do not try to figure out what it is like for you to not be there. Please do not try to make yourself disappear. Yes, you have no control over what happens, and hopefully you won't put in the effort I did for so long to find enlightenment. You don't have to do anything at all! Freeze! Nothing has you surrounded!

And just remember, all the angels will have a good laugh at your efforts after you die!

The Way of Nothing: Nothing in the Way

The character George Costanza from *Seinfeld* once summed up the show as being about nothing. In one episode, George attempts to pitch the show to the president of NBC, Russell. When Russell asks what kinds of stories will be in the show, George explains that there won't be any stories at all and that nothing happens. When Russell asks why anyone would watch the show, George can only reply, because it's on TV.

I think I also can sum up the show happening on earth with that one word, "Nothing!" Nothing is the secret to having a fulfilling life. This is the wisdom of nothing.

The way of nothing is a return to the simplicity of what is happening. The story is happening. You are watching it because it is happening; it is on TV right now. It does not matter what is on the show. Whether it is boring or entertaining or sad or happy, you have no choice but to watch it.

Right now what is on TV are these words being read. The words come out of nothingness and are being read by nothingness. You are not reading them as a separate individual. Reading is happening effortlessly without you. This is the way of nothing.

By trying to figure it out, you get in the way. But remember, there is already nothing in the way. You are free even before you look for freedom. That is the game of nothingness.

When you reappear, then you are part of the story on TV, which is still happening out of nothing. You simply become like the words you are reading. You are no different than the words on this page or the vibration of your thought as it happens seemingly inside your head. What is causing this thought? Is it me or you, or it is simply happening?

Duality happens when there is a sense of you reading, but this will disappear hundreds of times while reading this book. It disappears not because this material is any more special than that in a gossip magazine, but because you dissolve through resonance with what is the capacity for the words, ink, paper, thoughts, and sensations to appear. The capacity for resonance allows everything to happen spontaneously, and because of its ordinariness, this capacity remains unrecognised. It is like being unaware you are breathing or that your heart is beating, yet these functions are essential to your life. This nothingness is the only way awareness can enter the scene.

This capacity makes your heart beat and makes you breathe. Nothingness is breathing. In appearing to breathe it forgets itself and becomes alive in the story of you. This duality of nothing and something is happening within non-duality. This is evidence that all there is, is nothingness.

In non-duality or nothingness, everything seems to appear but is left alone, leaving nothing in the way of that oneness. When you are there, reality seems to split off into a something (you-centre) and whatever that new something is experiencing. This is the famous subject/object or context/content split. This new subject or new context is not real but notional. It is a conceptual subject that is in truth an object. This is proven by your being aware of it. Since the awareness can be aware of this conceptual subject (you-centre), this means that it is an object. Then we go further down the rabbit hole.

The funny part is that this new you actually believes it is a self-contained authority on what it experiences, yet it is also only part of the scenery happening in the pure subjectivity of nothingness. It is what is happening on TV, but suddenly you are a very real and central character. This phenomenon seems to put you in your own way of recognising what is. In fact, you are this phenomenon, so you don't see the reality and mystery of no-you. You believe you are the separate experiencer on TV.

The way of nothing has nothing to do with you as this separate experience, but this is not an unloving nothingness. It is not like being abandoned, although you might feel that way at times. It is fullness without end—pure love. It is pure love because it is undivided nothingness. This is nothing seeing everything as itself, which is the totality of unconditional love. The way of nothingness is not a cold void but a free wholeness in which all can and does apparently happen including the miraculous appearance of a separate you-centre. Again, this is in no way a negation of you; that would be pointless.

Nothingness is the essence of simplicity. The way is simple because it is no way. This path is obvious because there is no path and nowhere to go. If you think of it, it makes perfect sense. If all that exists is the infinite, then how much effort would it take to be that? Since it is what you are, in theory it would take *zero* effort. To be a separate you takes much more energy than to be what you truly are, which takes no effort at all.

Logically then, if you are not experiencing freedom, then you must be making something out of nothing. You are putting effort into what you are not, and this is how most of us live life. We complicate the way of nothing or no way by adding to the equation. We place objects to hide the subjectivity of what we are. Ultimately, the way of nothing reveals that even the objects are nothing. This is simple unity.

Nothing Moves

When you disappear completely, nothing moves. The stillness in its original nothingness is without any movement. This is always and eternally the case. Thoughts, feelings, sensations, the body, birds, trees, and clouds all appear to move. When we witness all this from a separate position of "me witnessing," there is a distinction between the me that sees and that which moves. In nothingness, though witnessing can come and go, there is no separate witness.

However, our eyes still see cars going by or birds flying. Objects continue to move, but the underlying principle of the infinite silence is seen without anyone separate to view it. This sounds a lot more complicated than it is. Actually, it happens often during the day, but because of the habit of self-identifying and self-referencing we don't see it clearly. Because of this simplicity, we don't see that nothing moves.

When there is simply nothingness, there is no longer a distinction between movement and that which watches the movement; the separate watcher disappears. In nothing, there is only what is, and this is unity. It's as simple as that.

We can spend years trying to see the awareness, be the awareness, or identify with it instead of the sense of self. We can try to see what it is that is witnessing. What is it that is aware? Is that me or pure awareness? How do I know? We can drive ourselves crazy trying to make these distinctions. As I said, we are already bananas. Why add to our insanity? My elementary teacher was right—keep it simple, silly.

Like a monkey gravitating to a banana, awareness moves naturally to that which it is attracted to. Awareness will naturally come to the stillness of nothing since nothingness is its source. Nothingness is delicious to attention. You already find nothingness more delicious than the mind or you would not be reading this book. It is a clear sign that you have the banana for your monkey mind.

Trying to control attention can be frustrating and is also not the way of nothing. Engaging your mental effort to control movement only causes more movement.

Moving from attention to movement and back to attention to what does not move reveals that nothing is in the way of oneness. Unity or oneness is seen in the simplicity and ease of nothing. Since there is nothing in the way, there is only freedom. What does this freedom look like with respect to movement?

From your perspective, it is preferable to have no movement at all. This is the underlying desire when sitting down to focus and meditate (if you are doing it). Stillness may not be the goal of the meditation itself, but we all want it because we recognise that our freedom lies in exploring that stillness.

You are completely right about wanting stillness, and being right is the problem. Many have spent their entire lives in caves in an intense effort to still the mind. What could be more important than discovering the source of stillness? It is easy to rationalise our efforts to still the mind.

Is it not worth all the effort in the world? Absolutely!

Do you need any effort at all? Absolutely not!

In the way of nothing, we already have all the stillness we can handle before we even begin to still the mind. This is the mystery of no-you. Congratulations—you already have it all!

Now I can hear you saying, "I do not have a still mind—quite the opposite—so how could that be true?" Of course you would say that—you are right, and you are the problem.

I invite you to look at this stillness from the perspective of what you already are, which has nothing in the way. Right now what there is, is nothingness. In this nothing there is no movement, only the allowance of movement. This is the difference between you and no-you! This is a very important concept to understand and a magnificent freedom if understood.

What you are—stillness without movement—allows everything to happen. This concept applies to everything but specifically to your relationship with the silence/freedom and thought/energy. The stillness, which is the background or screen of the movie of life, allows it all.

"You are already *still*," my teacher told me when the opposite was my experience. Being in my own way, I could not see it. All he did was keep pointing to it until eventually I lost myself enough to see that there is a heck of a lot of stillness already. The seeker you-centre is never okay with what it experiences. When we see this, we can allow it to do its dance since it is only another object of awareness.

Your thinking happens in this screen of nothing, as do your emotions. You yourself happen on this screen of nothing. You already are the absolute stillness, which *has* movement but is *not* movement.

What does the stillness do when there is movement? That's right, nothing!

When you are trying to be still and breathe to relax as the energy of anxiety pulses throughout your body, what does the stillness do? Nothing at all. I see a pattern unfolding.

When you scream and yell at nothingness and say, "Don't you care at all about what I'm going through to be free?" what do you hear? Silence.

Does it care about what happens? No.

Does this silence allow it all? Yes.

Has it ever not allowed it all? No.

The nothingness provides evidence that you are okay exactly as you are and that your story is also completely on track. You have made no wrong turns on the path; even the wrong turns were the right ones. Nothingness has an unconditional infinite love for you. This nothingness loves you as an appearance in a story and you as nothingness itself. This is the freedom of being exactly as you are!

Nothingness is the answer to your prayers and the secret to peace and contentment with your life and story as it unfolds. Waking up does not suddenly transform you into an invincible god that has no challenges or weaknesses. You would probably have to go to a cave to escape them, but you would still have you to contend with. Waking up means being humble enough to have problems without needing to fix them. Problems seem to solve themselves when we are out of the way.

Seeing that nothing is in your way and that allowing is the natural way of being makes life easy. Suddenly you see that you don't need to do anything because there is no you and no path you are required to walk on.

Indeed that little and big nothing is a great teacher. Listen to her unmoving stillness within you; she is the divine surprise.

All the great teachers rest in her silence.

Nothing Changes

The silence of self never changes, yet what we think we are changes and evolves all the time. The evolution of our changing identity is part of the story. The advanced or spiritual story is called "expanding consciousness."

Out of all the stories, this is my favourite one because it keeps on growing and changing forever. This ensures that I am on the path forever, expanding into infinity. The Zen question is who or what is it that is on this path?

This spiritual story is very appealing because it seems to ring true to our experience of waking up. But it is only an illusion that you evolve and change, and the spiritual ego hates this. This was the hardest pill for me to swallow because I was attached to this path and to being someone important on it.

I am not talking about rejecting the path we are on. I have nothing against it at all! This is the path of joy in which no path is *the path*. What I am saying is that identifying with the story of a me that is changing and evolving becomes harder to see. My sense is that the difficulty in seeing this relates to how close we are to the story of awakening. It can be a sensitive issue for some.

Our experience also seems to contradict the idea that nothing changes because as we "evolve" we get lovelier, more blissful, and better looking, which seems to be the proof that we are indeed evolving! Yes, our story is changing, but being has not changed at all.

We can fall in love with our spiritual story because it so beautiful. Don't get me wrong—this is not a bad place to be; but to see our changeless nature is to see this radiance in infinite ways.

Even after an experience of freedom, the seeking aspect of the you-centre can reappear to keep the momentum of seeking going. This is part of a very subtle dance of letting go and surrendering to what is beyond this little centre.

Some of us love to keep learning new tricks and techniques to stay on the cutting edge of consciousness. Instead of getting out of the way to see consciousness as nothingness, we keep adding to our storehouse of knowledge. We think that the more we understand, the more consciousness will expand. This simply confuses us, making us unable to see the natural simplicity of what is.

There is neither you nor your expanding consciousness. There is only nothing or consciousness as nothingness, which is the same as nothing at all. As you appear to fall away, it may seem that you are becoming wiser and have expanded. But this is true within the story only and can distract you from fully losing yourself in the silence. Don't settle for a more loving and evolved you because that you will die. It will die more loving than it was before, but you will be settling for less. Change always dies. Nothingness can't die because it doesn't change.

I remember being with my teacher and somebody was saying how nice I was. Everyone was calling me Sweet P, and I was feeling very proud and thought, "Yes they're right, I am nice." Then he said to me, "Yes, and at your funeral there will be lots of nice things said about you. That is not such a bad thing." At the time I thought he was agreeing with the person, but later I got it.

The teaching is eternal, so sometimes it takes a while (about eight years in my case) to sink in. So what that I seemed to be nice and sweet—who cares? That was a natural by-product of meditation and exploring the silence. Character sometimes changes for the better, which was happening for me. My teacher was pointing out that the true self is changeless. How the character *appears* is irrelevant, which is where the saying, "Grumpy before enlightenment, grumpy after enlightenment," comes in.

You want the whole enchilada, which includes all the extras

on the side. The extras are not the main dish of freedom. You may appear wiser and that your consciousness has expanded, but that has nothing to do with you. I get better looking every day, but that is just by the grace of God.

This appearance of change is entirely true of those who feel close to freedom (I don't mean getting better looking). We seem to be getting more conscious, but I assure you it is all a big joke. What you are has never changed, nor has it needed any experience to be more than what it already is.

So why do I keep needing more experiences to feel as if I am worthy? The only reason we all don't just pop into freedom now is that we believe we are unworthy of the full enchilada of enlightenment. We settle for scraps or for a continuing journey, compromising the only gift there is. Feeling unworthy is partly the fault of people like me using fancy words like "enlightenment" or "unlimited, infinite, radiant, all-encompassing, shining-out-of-your-eyes bliss." It sounds good.

Words like "unity," "freedom," "infinite," "God," and "supreme consciousness" all sound too big and far away. From the perspective of the you-centre, it's intimidating to think of becoming a sage. Who do you think you are to deserve the kingdom of Heaven? It really does sound too extravagant to achieve, doesn't it? No wonder we spend so much time and energy on the search. I believed I had a heck of a lot of fixing and purifying to do if I was to deserve enlightenment. I believed that it was more than a changeless, familiar nothingness.

Maybe you and I am not worthy of enlightenment, but what about nothing? Are we worthy of nothing? Let's consider it.

Being worthy of nothing sounds more attainable and requires no change at all. Nothingness is the way of truth. The term "nothing" used in this context is the same as God, the infinite, and radiant, dazzling bliss. This is the surprise of nothingness! It is an appropriate term to describe what we are because we require nothing more to be worthy of what does not change. The way of nothing is changeless, and therefore all change is only a reflection of that nothingness. Your essence is changelessness.

Isn't it interesting that we spend so much time investing in change and so little in what is changeless? Change seems necessary because you think you can't have freedom as you are now. You are not good enough. You will never be good enough. Despite all the investment of energy, money, and time, nothing has changed in reality. The bad news is that after spending twenty years meditating, you are no closer to freedom. The good news is that the you-centre is irrelevant to freedom. In the way of nothing, there is no you except the changing story of you.

By all means work on your image, update your Facebook page, and for goodness' sake take the spinach out of your teeth. There is nothing wrong with that. But understand that what you truly are *is* the unchangeable, not the image in the story.

A more awake you is no freer than an ignorant you. You have no influence over the silence and nothing to do with what is changeless. Thank God for that. Can you imagine if it was up to us to get free? Talk to me in a million years.

We are all in the process of change. Change works for most things in the world, such as achieving material success. In that sphere, we can play and adapt to bring abundance. But change does not work for the way of nothing.

The more you change in life, the more the you-centre changes; this happens as part of the story. Ironically, when you fail and go backwards in life, this often seems to bring you closer to what your heart wants. Nobody in their right mind wants to fail, but failure seems to lead to success in terms of dissolving or expanding into freedom. That these changes often lead to a leap into the unknown are a testament to the fact that you inevitably recognise that there is no you choosing your fate. That nobody is running the show is liberating but can be initially scary.

Thanks to God, nothing has ever happened. This does not

mean that we have to feel like failures for wasting so much time but that we can have a good laugh ourselves. We are simply divine entertainment and nothing else.

The Fear of Nothingness

Why not start at the end of everything?

To have eternal peace, we must be willing to face the fear of death. This fear of death includes not only the fear of losing our body, but also more intimately the fear of losing the you-centre we cherish so much. It seems terrible to think of losing this precious gift of me that the universe has blessed us with, but this gift has only ever been on loan.

We rely on this sense of self as if it is a permanent gift, but that is the biggest lie, and one we always overlook. We would rather do anything than look into ourselves and face our fear. We are fooling ourselves, and instead of appreciating being alive we are living as if we were dead. We have everything backwards.

The fear of death or nothingness is really a fear of nothing much at all. It seems like a huge obstacle to overcome, but we are projecting about what we think nothingness or death is like. Students report that "crossing that river" or "jumping off that cliff" into the unknown is not as big a deal as they thought. (I don't mean literally jumping off a cliff but an inner jump). The only thing the inner jumpers or crossers can say to you is, "Jump! It's okay!" Is this easier said than done? The thing is, we never know what dissolving into the silence is like until we try it.

It only takes a second to realise that everything you thought concerning what you are is a lie. The obviousness of this truth threatens your identity, but you wouldn't be interested in this book if you didn't have the courage to look into the heart of it all.

The zombie apocalypse is already happening; everyone is walking around as if dead or in a dream. Wake up! Get out of your trance for a second and really see. What are you looking out of? Could it be that nothing you have ever stood for or thought about has any significance at all? Is that a sad or a liberating concept?

Even all the epiphanies and revelations you've ever had are gone. If you have had the experience of waking up, it is gone. If you were enlightened and fell asleep again, becoming a poor separate human, that is also gone now. Even your enlightenment is gone into nothingness. You have to start all over now! Is that a sad or a liberating concept?

Nothingness is so huge it even swallows up our experience of freedom. What is left? All those wonderful spiritual moments of joy and bliss are gone. Nothing is left. That nothingness is the point of no return that we cannot escape. Just like death and taxes, it is the only way. The inevitable nothingness gobbles us up. All you can do is delay your peace, and while that may seem like an option for some people, for you it is not.

I used to say that God had me by the cashews because it felt as if there was no option for me; I had to find out the truth or die. A pressure was pushing me to seek. Even though I thought it was all about me, looking back I see that it was an impersonal push over the cliff to the unknown. Have you felt it?

Underneath this pressure is a fire of love for the silence, a desire to unite with the beloved. How far are we willing to go? I am not talking about physically jumping off a building or a bridge but maybe something psychologically equivalent.

There is a cliff that we do not want to jump over. We are aware of this in the quietest moments when nothing is happening. We want to distract ourselves with anything to stop us from falling off the edge. In the mystery of no-you, we have a silent yearning to jump off this cliff and unite with the divine. Perhaps we fear a loss of identity. Who am I if I let go into nothingness? And what will happen to me?

I can't answer this. Nobody can make the jump for you, maybe not even you. Some students report surprise and say, "What was I so scared of?" When you turn on the light in a dark room, you see there is no monster after all and no reason to be afraid.

The greatest bliss comes from surrendering into the unknown—the death of everything about you. The good news is that by taking the plunge into the sea, anything that is real will stick around.

That which is real stays after this inner death because it is real. This is very obvious. Truth is true, and reality is real. You cannot be born, and you cannot die. This is a simple concept. What do you have to lose? Time is ticking away, and here we are wasting it by chatting. Instead let's do it! It's a good day to die!

Big-Self-Absorption

Why not focus our attention on the big Self instead of the small one?

Waking up is ridiculously simple because it is only about where we focus our attention. All our seeking, practising, and effort comes to rest in that simple knowingness. If I focus my attention on the little self, then that becomes real to consciousness. If I focus it on the big self, then that becomes real to consciousness. Consciousness is like a magnifying glass; what you focus attention on grows beneath this clear glass.

When we starve consciousness through not thinking, the glass has no choice but to see itself. Without objects, the subject sees that it is the source of the attention and consciousness comes home to its true nature. We wake up through what we focus on. In essence, we are no different from this magnifying glass.

If we really knew what this big Self was, we would all gladly focus our attention there. This is where words become pointers to truth but not truth itself. Nobody can give you the truth through words, but maybe the resonance behind them will cause an energetic shift to happen.

Instead of talking, the great sages rely on resting in the silence as the teaching. Their magnifying glasses are sharply focused on the nothingness. This gives them the widest possible view, a view that can take everything in spontaneously without being distracted.

Discovering the silence is about resonating in the teaching of nothingness. The teacher is no one, and the student is no one. Together they are one making up the way of nothing. The teaching is there to show the student that there is nothing in the way. Once this is understood, the sky is the limit, and we can fly.

Regardless of the specifics of the teaching, showing you that you are divine and do not need to be fixed is the ultimate goal.

It may sound irreverent to speak of the teacher and the teaching as nothingness. This relationship is the most sacred of relationships because it is based on the divine. Nothingness is sacred, and perceiving it as otherwise shows only a superficial understanding of the word "nothing."

The teaching of nothingness points the way to clarity. Knowing this helps you to lose your fixation on what changes and moves. This silent resonance provides the necessary fertile ground of emptiness for awakening to happen spontaneously. This is the sacredness of nothing.

If we can discover the wonder of focusing attention on nothing (or stillness) then we can allow nothingness to reveal itself as all that is. Ultimately, the nothingness appears to move and change. The way of nothing moves the attention to itself so we have less interest in what comes and goes within the show. Eventually, in big-Self-absorption you see your small self in the same light as what comes and goes. Nothing dramatic needs to happen; it can be as simple as enjoying a cup of tea. Every act can be and is the act of absorption in the silence.

However, this big Self doesn't seem to offer us much when we compare it to the small one. It seems as if we have to give up everything just for the hope that something wonderful might happen to our you-centre. After all, the big Self is just nothingness. But what if we gave up everything and nothing happened? Since the little me can't even be there to enjoy being the Self what is the point of focusing our attention there? What will it give us?

The way of nothing is a continual exploration of the big Self, which at first can seem ordinary and dull. It might even seem crazy to focus attention on nothing, since it doesn't exactly have the attractiveness of Disneyland, Vegas, or of any of the many thoughts or emotions that could be passing by. The only time we might treasure the big Self is in the moments of torment and chaos when we reach out to go to our "happy place."

Through falling into this silence, however, a natural magnetic pull begins to happen spontaneously that becomes increasingly more enjoyable. The mind starts to desire to take a rest from activity and stay in the quiet. This quiet is the throne of the mind and the source of love. The mind that we have become so accustomed to identifying with has been tamed and loses its grip on attention as it falls into the source of its own reality.

This mind is another concept that appears out of nothingness. We all assume we have a mind and talk about it as if it is obvious, saying things like, "What's on your mind?" "My mind is driving me crazy!" and "I'm going out of my mind!" On inspection, we see the mind as another piece of content appearing out of nowhere. Through big-Self-absorption, all concepts are swallowed up in the inevitable sea of nothingness.

As the concepts fall away, we have a gentle curiosity about what is left for the light of attention to expose. The content of the mind becomes subtler and subtler as awareness moves into the sea of what we think we are. This can be very intimidating because it can seem like an impenetrable wall of "I am not going anywhere." Because of a tight knot or a subtle holding on, the identity resists dissolving.

The important point is that it all happens out of nothingness, and there is literally nothing in the way. Seeing an obstacle in the mind/identity to overcome is happening to the you-centre only. Remember that you are exploring the mystery of no-you, although that is of little comfort when you feel stuck and think you are suffering. You just might need a hug and some encouragement from the wise people you surround yourself with. (I hope you do that!)

As attention dives into the nothingness (big-Self-absorption), we see the things we need to let go of. In the way of nothing, the only reason we see anything is so that it can be allowed. Allowing is the only job of attention.

More often than not, before we even become aware of what

we were holding onto, it will have disappeared into the nothingness. This process is a magical adventure that continually reveals subtle ideas and thoughts that we had believed were real. It is a wonder to see them at a distance and to know that they have no power anymore.

During this dance we see a parrot that constantly comments, a judge that judges, and a controller that tries to control. We see a carnival of crazy characters playing their specific roles to the letter. We need to see them there playing to understand that they are just thoughts, and they are only doing their job the best they can. Go ahead and thank them for their good work. To see them is liberating since they have run our lives for so long. We think we are literally these voices inside our heads. Once we see this carnival for what it is, our view expands, providing instant insight.

That being said, it is my experience that most students usually have specific thoughts that will continue to come up, along with the intense emotion they are attached to. Anxiety was my specific thought. The energy, which I labelled as anxiety, was not the issue—the thoughts surrounding it were the problem. The energy itself was actually an innocent movement. One day I saw that the same energy I had labelled as anxiety my whole life was actually bliss. This tells us that the mind is not an accurate judge of energy.

These specific thoughts seem to pull all our attention, as if we are being sucked out of nothingness back into the very real and personal you-centres with our stories surrounding those centres. In moments where we lose our attention, it helps to see that it is not about us. In our stories, we will fight until the way of nothing has more appeal than the struggle. The good news is that in most stories about us, these specific thoughts get easier to laugh at or at least to not take so seriously.

When we can let go of the special thoughts, everything else is a piece of cake. Over and over, realisation becomes clearer and clearer, and eventually only the simplicity of attention is left. It dawns on us in the way of nothing, that what matters is where the attention is. At first it is all about you and where you focus your attention, but then as your attention is refined and absorbed into nothingness, the nothing itself becomes the attention, and the effortful game of *your* attention is over.

What is left after you are gone is only nothing and everything, which is big-Self-absorption. This is like resting in active alertness in all there is. Everything else continues to play and dance, trying to entice this attention back to the enjoyment of the play. The anchor of nothingness, however, allows attention to enjoy the play without getting lost in being a separate you again. If you do get lost, it gets easier to see. In the way of nothing it is always easier because of the momentum of the path of joy.

It seems strange that nobody actually knows that they have a choice as to where they focus their attention. We live life more often than not on autopilot or auto-puppet as we move from one thought or feeling to the next, feeling like victims of whatever is arising for us. What if the part of us that is allowing all this actually contains the secret to freeing us from this victimhood? The part that is allowing this is already completely free as it is.

The source of our wandering attention is attention itself, but that simply goes on unnoticed because of our constant attraction to the movement, which leads to constant distraction from reality. We all have attention deficit disorder because we are unable to stop moving from object to object. We are unable to see the source of our own attention that is the underlying primary principle of life itself. Inability to focus is only a habit we have picked up. How can we ever hope to focus and be still without recognising the subjectivity of that attention?

The whole point of exploring the mystery of no-you is that in nothingness, attention is unwaveringly one-pointed. It is this single focus that makes life easy.

The attention does not know itself as the context in which all of this is occurring. This is part of the play of your story or your attention on the story. Once you acquire a natural awareness of nothingness, you focus the attention powerfully in one direction. This is the key to freedom. When the attention, like a bunny, can remain still without hopping from carrot to carrot, it can reveal the way of nothing effortlessly. The bliss bunny just wants to hop.

The wondrous thing is that we have had this magical magnifying glass in our hands the entire time. It remained hidden from us like some secret treasure, but then one day almost by accident we saw that the key to our joyful freedom was the simplicity of being actively alert now. This was always the case; we just didn't see it that way.

What can we see with this attention right now? Let's find out! What does not move or change within what we are seeing or experiencing?

Beyond the concept of duality or non-duality is the conceptless, free oneness, which contains nothing but the nakedness of attention on itself. This attention is the natural gift we have been given to explore what is true about this instant. Absolutely nothing is hidden from our attention. The more we practise being actively alert to the now, the more we realise the treasure of silence, and the easier we find the journey into the unknown.

A side effect of discovering the attention of nothingness is that the mind tends to slow down. Due to the magnifying nature of nothingness, the underlying silence of unity is more obvious without attention on the monkey mind.

This results in joy, bliss, and contentment.

Who? What?

Why not discover who or what ultimately is there?

To be truly satisfied so that we are desire-less, we need to be content with who and what we are. When I refer to desire-less, what I mean is being content in the nothingness that has no desires. This does not mean trying to stop natural desires; you cannot do this. To rest in the desire-less is to automatically allow desires without resistance. Being in nothingness is intensely joyful because there is nothing else you could possibly desire.

A so-called liberated being can and usually does have the same desires as a so-called separate being. The difference between a separate being and a sage is that the latter does not attach her identity to desires. Since there is no longer a you-centre, the desires come and go. What remains is the resting in desire-lessness. Anthony de Mello refers to the barrier to freedom as attachment-desire. It is clear that desire itself is not bad but a necessary part of the human condition, and nothing needs to be done with it. Nothingness is delicious because there are no attachment desires in pure experiencing.

As long as we are looking outside ourselves to find what we are, we cannot be satisfied, at least not permanently. But this is more than the intellect can comprehend and requires us to surrender our understanding of how we think things work to fully know who or what we are. The way things actually are is usually the opposite of what we think they are.

What we call this "whatness" is irrelevant; the important point is that we move into the direct knowingness of it. The paradox of this quest, however, is that anything we know can only be an object because there must be a knower of the known. This is a classic subject-object duality that leads to the question: Who or what wants to know? In ancient texts this paradox is referred to as the eye that cannot see itself. In Zen it is the original face that you have never seen.

What is direct knowingness? For who or what does this direct knowingness occur?

Many students of the way of nothing agree that the further they travel along the way, the less they know. This path is more about not knowing than knowing. But to the outsider looking at them, these students seem to know more than we do. Sages often seem to have something we don't, but the opposite is true. They have no special knowledge, yet they remain in a kind of divine certainty in what is unknown.

When there is no longer an identity that desires to attain more knowledge, there is a certainty in the pure subjectivity without a desire to know. For simplicity, we could call this a knowing of nothingness or an empty knowing where there is no you that knows. What do you want to know when there is only THIS? (This meaning subjectivity of nothingness).

There is no sense of a missing piece of the puzzle. In my experience, there was always something missing. At times I would look outside myself to the sage to retrieve that missing piece. "If only I could see it, I would be free," I would think. Then the sage would patiently point back to nothingness.

As long as we have questions, they need to be answered; this is part of awakening. But that part of us that is trying to figure it out is eventually seen for what it is and disappears. In my own case, I was unaware that I was still trying to figure it out. Even though I was almost free or big-Self-absorbed, I could not see that I was still figuring things out in my head. Then it was plainly pointed out to me that even though I was having a nice experience, I was still thinking and missing something.

I understood, and since then have never tried to figure it out. I experienced an energetic recognition that nothingness itself was sufficient, and the desire to know something other than nothingness fell away. I already had everything I was looking for, and the missing piece was only a figment. In this nothingness, the

Self is content with nothing but the Self, so there is no sense of anything missing—only completeness.

Through grace or luck, that desire to know becomes less important than resting in the quiet unknown. Before this change, the unknown was either scary because there was nothing to hold onto or it seemed like just a boring nothingness. But it becomes alive with the unending mystery of what we are. When that question, "What am I?" is posed to the nothing, there is silence. Could it be that simple? Maybe silence was the answer all along.

The mind wants to know. This knowing is only a part of the story and our fascination with content. Even non-duality these days is full of concepts, and I must confess that everything I could write is also a concept and not the actual way of nothing. I can only do my best to point to it.

Through big-Self-absorption we discover that infinity is actually quite big, as physics continually shows. One day a physicist friend of mine told me that theoretically anything that we can imagine about the multi-dimensional nature of what we are must be possible because the infinite has infinite potential. At first I disagreed because I was holding onto a position of there being only nothingness. When I saw what I was doing, I laughed because the position appeared so big as to be an absolute truth. But in the way of nothing, there are no absolute truths; they are reserved for the individual. When the position disappeared, however, the nothingness seemed even greater than before, which is humbling. Now there is even less to know.

When talking about omniscience, which is the all-knowingness mentioned in the Vedas, Ramana Maharishi reportedly said that the Vedas only mention omniscience to attract people who are looking for knowledge as an object to search for God. But God knows nothing. This is the ultimate bait and switch.

Can you imagine if you knew everything? It would be like

having the entire contents of the Internet downloaded in your head. Nobody needs to know anything anymore—just Google it!

The Heart of Openness

Only by staying completely empty can the heart open up to the eternal oneness of its nature. When, how, or even if this openness *really* occurs is a mystery. Consider yourself lucky if it does happen, as it is pretty rare.

Often the greatest tragedies of life can break down the old structures we held in place, opening up a fresh aliveness. When the time comes, ripeness opens the heart up to a new way of being. Usually, this happens not by choice but when we least expect it.

The worst and greatest moment of my life happened simultaneously when my girlfriend of many years left me. I felt complexly stripped of my identity. The whole time I was enmeshed in co-dependency, and suddenly I had no idea who I was anymore. My whole life was about her. My heart was ripped open, and although I was devastated, openness to the universe rushed in. Now I had new eyes to see with. I was suddenly aware of other people besides me and her.

This was the grace of the way of nothing. I was in the way, and instead of living the rest of my life like that, I was taken out the way. What did I do for this to happen? Nothing. All I had was an intense desire for freedom, but even that was not my choice. Never in a million years would I have ended that relationship; I would have chosen to be stuck forever. This identity (and I assume the identity of many) would have chosen being stuck over being free. But it is nobody's choice! When your number is up, all you can do is go the easy way or the hard way. Hopefully, you are open enough to pick the easy way.

This openness flowers not only in tragedy but in meditation when you dissolve in the silence or when you are enjoying your favourite moment. Suddenly everything is open to explore, and nothing is in the way of being.

Whenever we hold onto anything, no matter how enlightened or divine it may seem to us, it removes us from reality. Of course there is only oneness that holds nothing in the first place, but as long as that is not our experience it helps to keep emptying the cup. By emptying the cup, we see that nothing is in the way at all.

The recognition that nothing is in the way is freedom and the cosmic duh! When realising that nothing is in the way, many students are amazed that they had never seen it before. It is so obvious that nothing can obscure it, and it seems astonishing that it was not seen before. I remember actually being shocked that not everyone in the world was experiencing this nothingness. The miracle was no longer about freedom but about something so obvious appearing so elusive. Nothingness really does a good job of being something-ness! The magic of attention is that it keeps the you-centre fascinated with everything except the reality of nothing at all.

The spiritual path is full of concepts. All paths are full of concepts. Everything that is not the way of nothing, or whatever you choose to call the no-path (I call it a path of joy) is a concept. By holding onto concepts, the you stays more or less closed to the aliveness of nothing. As long as the heart is even a little closed, it is not satisfied and will continue to wander the desert to fill that hole. The way of nothing creates wholeness, leaving the naked simplicity of what is.

Whatever we believe about freedom keeps us one step removed. This includes the way of nothing, which cannot be turned into a concept except by you. You are the only one who can turn the nothing into a something, at which point it ceases being the way of nothing. Yet that no-path of nothing is all there is and the final door to dissolving the greatest concept of all— you.

Some inspiring non-dualists have a fear of dualism. Who cares if you are dualistic or not? Only when we waste our time thinking about it does it matter. The truth is that there is only the emptiness of reality that is also full and complete. In the way of nothing, nobody is more non-dual because there is nobody at all.

The statement that the self is both emptiness and fullness is dualistic and not what we experience non-dually in nothingness; they are only words, and they mean absolutely nothing. Every single word or idea in this book means nothing! They only point to what is entirely beyond conceptualisation.

Experiencing emptiness and fullness is another subject (*the* subject) altogether. This happens without anyone to experience in nothingness. Emptiness and fullness are experienced as a complete whole, a Happy Meal, so to speak.

Anytime you claim anything as truth, you are immediately in your own way. This is something we love to do along the way to our enlightenment. If I told you all the times I thought I was enlightened, you would probably laugh at me. Underlying all those revelations was nothingness—I was not there. There was freedom in that instant since there was nothing in the way, but then I got excited, saying to myself, "This is it—I got it! Good for me!" Or else I'd say, "Oh shit, I lost it. I had it, now where is it?"

The heart allows and accepts everything to come and go no matter what it is. By being open, the way is clear for a path of joy and greater ease and simplicity. Nothing is more valuable than the peace of being open. Until then, we will keep putting our hand in the fire. Ouch!

In the way of nothing, no label or statement is absolutely true. By clinging to what we feel is true, it takes on an apparent reality. This gets subtler as we continue to explore the mystery of no-you. Whenever you are taking something seriously, you are there. It is amazing how serious we can become about nothing at all. Seriously!

It's a Good Day to Die!

Curiosity killed the cat ... meow, scratch, scratch.

Most people don't understand the joy behind the statement, "It's a good day to die." It reflects a great attitude of open, fearless adventurousness. It says, "Let's go straight into the unknown and see what treasure we can find." Like children we go into the cave or forest because we sense something magnificent just beyond our reach. Nobody needs to push us, least of all ourselves. All that happens in nothingness is curiosity.

What you are is so much bigger than you think. You are simply a divine mystery to me and everyone else. All you can do is play with the innocence of a child (or a cat) to discover that cave or mystical forest of no-you. Ultimately, nothing is there but being in the forest of mystery. This may be the end of the story of you and your past, but it is the beginning of your magical life. Life has just begun, but for real this time. Before, we were just pretending to live, going through the motions like an old auto-puppet. Now the cosmic adventure has begun, and every moment is a new beginning.

The way of nothing is not a dry way but an infinite fountain of unending concept-free bliss. Instead of chasing after a drop, we find an ocean of alive-bliss capturing our attention. What do we need to do to maintain this state? That's right—nothing.

This does not mean we stop pretending. Actually, we can truly pretend because there is no way that we need to be. We are listening to the silence while playing our part. There is no defined form this takes; the silence can take any form. What form are you going to take next?

Without you in the way, the adventure takes on a new kind of story in which you could say you are like a puppet or a cartoon character in a show. You are still the star but are no longer distracted by your stardom. That character is a puppet with all the same characteristics as before, such as your unique personality or my good looks!

Maybe by exploring the mystery of no-you, you get a few new upgrades (or maybe not) like a bigger smile or better attitude toward your partner. But even that is irrelevant to the wonder of this new stillness of no-you.

The Nothingness Meditation

Imagine that there is nothing. How long can you be okay with nothing at all? This meditation is designed to help you find out.

Don't be fooled by its apparent simplicity. As a child you were a lot better at meditating, so now it might take a little practice.

What is nothing? Find out through exploration.

What does nothing feel like?

What does nothing sound like?

Play with exploring this nothingness, and see how long you can stay aware of nothing. Maybe a second at first?

This meditation helps to open you up to the nothingness and create a relationship with what is already free. Nothingness is already free. Let it show you what that freedom is like. Let it teach you and guide you. Let it show you that you know absolutely nothing!

This nothingness will help you easily and effortlessly discern what is real from what is not. The key is the joy of exploration.

The Game of Death Meditation

What were you before you were born?
—Nisargadatta Maharaj

Here are some simple instructions to have a death before you die physically. Some of these things have really helped me to put things in perspective, especially when I was going through some rough times.

Did you know that of the seven or so billion people on the planet, none will be here in 120 years? Isn't that amazing? Even though our time here is very short relative to the age of the planet, we take things very seriously and personally. I did the arithmetic, and we are here for about .000000026 per cent of the life of the planet. This universe is even older.

We all act as if we are going to be here forever, and yet our bodies are fragile and vulnerable to disappearing. At any moment, that's it—you're done. You die all the time anyway without knowing it, so why not see no-you and free yourself of you if you can. Of course it's just a game because you can't do it.

To see that your essence is immortal is the wisest thing you can do while you are here. This is exploring the mystery of no-you. By dissolving yourself through meditation or dying on purpose (consciously not identifying with the separate self), the way of nothing opens up. What you are is immortal, but how can you know that while you identify with the separate you-centre that you think you are? Don't forget that this is a path of joy, so don't take it seriously.

As intelligent human beings, should we really be investing so much time and energy in what is temporary? Think about it! I remember as a child thinking it was very strange to go to university, get a good education, save lots of money working until I was sixty-five and then after retirement was over wait for death. I was going through a philosophical/existential phase, I guess.

My father was a construction supervisor for a company that builds multi-million-dollar custom homes. Every once in a while he brought me to the site to show me all the amazing homes. They were all so majestic and unique. As we were walking around, he would give me random facts about the home. "See that door? [it was huge hand-carved antique wooden door that opened into a yoga room]. They shipped it from India. See all the windows? It costs $400,000 just for the windows." It was another world, and I would imagine myself living in these mansions and wonder about the kind of people who could afford these places. It was Calgary, so usually the answer was oil.

Then one day he showed me one of the homes under construction. It was a nice home but modest in comparison with some. As we were walking around, he gave me all the facts: "The wires for the electrical and electronics alone cost $60,000 dollars." Then he began to tell me the story about the owners. The husband was a successful engineer who was building a dream home in which he and his wife would retire. He was sixty-five years old and had worked very hard his whole life to be able to have this home that had an elevator in it and a TV in the bathroom mirror so he could watch the soccer game while shaving.

Soon after they had begun the construction of his dream home, he died and his wife was talking over finishing building it. This story resonated deep within me; I had that same curiosity I'd as a child, and I never forgot the message: invest in or focus your attention on what is permanent. Act as if it's the last day of your life!

Let's protect our bodies and take our Chinese herbs, but let's also put energy into what is eternal, not in what is temporary. We need to know for sure that our attention is on what is immortal. I am not talking about undergoing physical death, which will happen naturally for all of us some day. I am talking about diving and dying into the aliveness to see what is eternal. It's a good day to die!

A billion years from now will any of this matter at all? Even in 120 years, it won't matter. So let's begin.

The best way to die is quickly, so don't delay it and suffer. Like putting a suffering cat to sleep, it is just the right thing to do. We are going to put you out of your misery quickly, like ripping off a Band-Aid.

Start by getting comfortable. Be okay with and notice the sensations in your body, whether they are excitement about death, being afraid to lose yourself, or simply the silence of nothing. You can usually pick your separate self up when you are done with the meditation, but I cannot promise you that. When Ramana Maharishi did this exercise, the sense of separation did not come back. So do not do it unless you are willing to die. Instead, just read through it but don't actually try it! Here we go.

There is nothing left, you are gone. You have died. You have nothing. You are holding nothing because there is no longer a you there. There are no thoughts or feelings. Simply notice what it is like to no longer have anything left at all. Nothing is yours anymore, and no sensations are yours.

What is happening now has nothing to do with you because you are not here. You can no longer control what is happening. Take this moment to notice that what is happening right now is happening without you there anymore to control it.

Now, with nothing in your way, does it matter whether or not you are there?

In the way of nothing, you are an appearance that comes and goes. In nothingness you are everything that comes and goes.

The meditation is the attention on what does not move or change. You do not have to do anything in this attention. Awareness is already aware! What is the awareness, without you, aware of now?

Notice that nothing is there to care about what the awareness is aware of now. Again, nothing needs to happen. There are no rules or expectations for you in this meditation because you are gone. Who or what would care about the experience in this meditation?

If nothing is happening, you are doing well.

If nothing is happening and thinking happens, that is nothing thinking, and you are doing well.

If you feel joy for no reason at all, then nothingness is joyful, and you are doing well.

If you smile at nothing, that is nothingness smiling, and you are doing well.

If you feel afraid, then nothingness is afraid, and you are doing well.

If you can't stand this meditation and just want a beer or coke to take the edge off, then nothingness can't stand this meditation and wants a beer or a coke, and you are doing well.

You cannot do this meditation wrong because there is no you. Nothingness is what moves and changes in your meditation practice and has nothing to do with you.

Nothingness is doing well! Keep up the good work!

If I've Died, How Can I Enjoy
This Cup of Coffee?

Nothingness is the ultimate enjoyer of everything! Without you, life and everything in it just tastes better, including the appearance of the you-centre and your story, whenever they pop up in consciousness.

To review: there are two basic fundamental truths (concepts) that become one (disappear in nothingness) though big-Self-absorption.

These truths are that nothingness moves and nothingness is *what* moves. They apply to everything in the way of nothing and merge into all there is. All that exists is nothingness and the appearance of nothing moving.

So the question is, if I've died, how can I enjoy this cup of coffee?

Traditionally, within a Zen or non-dual framework we would ask who or what died and who or what is drinking the coffee. To me these questions tend to engage the mind of a student, but I suppose it depends on which student's mind that is.

If all that exists is the infinite, then it is logical to assume that the infinite is enjoying the cup of coffee through this puppet body. To simplify, nothingness or no one enjoys the cup of coffee, and nothingness *is* what enjoys it.

The you-centre automatically assumes that you are the doer, mover, and enjoyer, but what enjoys is the infinite, which does not need a separate you to enjoy anything. Living like this allows for a richness beyond what happens when you are the one in charge of this centre.

Let's face facts—this centre is small. Not that there is anything wrong with being small. But what if that identification with the centre limits enjoyment? What if life is unending enjoyment, and we are living in a kind of Heaven? If it is true that enjoyment is the natural way of nothing, then nothingness is enjoying every-thing all the time because it is pure bliss. This bliss is nothingness.

Even a war is happening in nothing. The war itself doesn't make nothingness happy, but the essence of nothingness enjoys the root of every appearance, not the appearance itself. This makes the appearance of events irrelevant, resulting in bliss despite what happens. Wars are not fun for separate individuals, but watching them on TV changes them to impersonal events. The nothingness is not invested in events as they happen; it is always in bliss. This bliss is the potential for everyone when the personal gives way to impersonal nothingness.

I know what you are thinking. What about all the most terrible things in the world? Yes, what about them? Good and bad happen in a world of duality. The question is whether you are focusing your attention on the root or the appearance. And if these terrible things are not happening to you specifically, why would you give them attention? That choice just adds to your own drama and does not contribute to solving the problem. Choosing *your* peace is the only answer!

Uncaused Joy

I am not lazy, I am just happy doing nothing.
—message on a T-shirt

Uncaused joy is the bliss of nothingness. To be happy for no reason is evidence of freedom from the mind, which continually postpones joy. The mind says, "If I get this or that, then I'll be happy." What we really want is to be joyful all the time without any conditions.

There is nothing to it. It is simply a matter of seeing that in the absence of you; you had what you wanted all along. You are the only one keeping you from unadulterated blissfulness.

The first instruction I received from a teacher was, *"You don't need to think anymore—thinking disturbs your bliss."* This is the entire teaching wrapped up in a nice sentence.

Uncaused joy is contagious because it is endlessly laughing at nothing at all. Have you ever been so full of joy you laughed at nothing? Perhaps someone asked you, "What are you laughing at?" and you replied, "Nothing—really! I'm laughing at nothing at all." Nothing *is* funny! What's wrong with being happy for no reason? Think about it!

You do not need a reason to be happy and content in you life! You do not need to wait until anything becomes better. Waiting until you get a better job, relationship, house, or more money is investing in the temporary and will only lead to temporary happiness if any.

It is really funny if you consider the time and energy we put into achievements in order to be happy. It is not that the time is wasted on achievements themselves; they are part of life and necessary for survival sometimes. What is funny is seeking our happiness in these achievements because it can take years or decades to get what we want. When we get it, we have a brief moment of joy. How long does it last?

Before long, we are unsatisfied again but only because we have returned from our disappearance after achieving what we wanted. This disappearance is the you-centre achieving its illusion of happiness. When it gets what it wants, such as the gold medal or the new video game, it is briefly tranquilised, but like a raging addict it comes back for more, wanting the next thing. This cycle is familiar for everyone. We are all insane addicts looking for the next hit so we can enjoy our fleeting reward.

Pray that you don't get what you want out of life. If you don't, the search for something greater will begin. Failure is the greatest achievement you can hope for. Until you are free, hope for failure because then you can have all the illusions you desire without any side effects. Failure is the route to achieving bliss. Success only leads to the desire for greater achievements leading to greater success, and then you die unsatisfied.

By failing, you see that life doesn't work when you are running the show. "Okay, I get it," you say, "I will surrender into the way of nothing, and instantly have bliss. This is a path of joy. Life on the outside looks kind of crazy, but here I am, happy. Strange, isn't it? I should be unhappy, but I'm not." Because of "I'm not," you're happy, and now that you are not there, there is only the joy of nothing. Now you can have what you want without consequences or symptoms of withdrawal.

The amazing thing is that if you are attentive to nothing long enough and you are not in the way, life on the outside will get pretty sweet. Life will be greater than you ever could imagine because if there is one rule other than no rule, it is that your story looks better the more you are out of the way. It might take a little time because things seem to take longer in the "real world," but it is the safest investment you can make.

Bliss is supreme nothingness. Bliss does not move or change. The way of nothing is the way of bliss because they are the same thing. You cannot have nothingness without bliss. If you are still there controlling the process of freedom, then you may have ideas about what it is like to experience bliss. You might say, "I don't experience bliss—there is only nothing or stillness." Hogglewash!

You are bliss—end of story!

Satchitananda is Nothingness

The term *satchitananda* gives the quality-less nothing something the mind can comprehend. This description sums up the Happy Meal the nothingness served up for us to chew on.

Sat is the stillness and silence, the unmoving background or the screen of nothingness.

Chit is attention and alertness, the awareness of the screen of nothingness and everything moving on the screen.

Ananda is bliss, peace, and love, the sweetness of the screen of nothing and the enjoyment of everything moving on the screen.

The nothingness has also been referred to as *turiya* in Sanskrit, which means the fourth state, but is not really a state at all since it does not come and go. All states come and go in the infinite silence of being. *Turiya* is the source of all the arising states of consciousness. As the attention rests on that field of stillness, we discover that in an alert awareness of nothingness the states of waking, dreaming, and sleep subside and arise. This fourth state is also *satchitananda*, the missing state of consciousness, that, for whatever reason, we were not taught about in school.

I remember getting punished for resting in this state of nothingness. Kids were waving their hands in front of me as I was staring off into space. "Hello, is anybody there? What are you staring at?" they would say. They were making fun of me for not being there. Or the teacher would say, "Pay attention." The problem was, I paying attention to the wrong thing, but it was not my fault because there is a natural desire to rest there. We are not trained in how to pay attention to the fourth state of nothingness, which is probably why I got in trouble for daydreaming. (Fogging out or daydreaming happens as the mind loses its alertness in the silence. By being active in exploring this stillness, fogging out tends to happen less and less).

I also got in trouble for laughing too much in school. Has that ever happened to you? We were trying so hard not to laugh, it was hurting. I didn't even know why I was laughing. Trying to stop it makes it worse, and we got kicked out of class. This is why now I'm so scared to go to funerals.

As a child I began to feel very uncomfortable with silence on the inside and the outside. I was afraid that silence would indicate I was being weird, not fitting in, or being judged as stupid. I was labelled as too quiet or an introvert. People have difficulty with resting in nothingness. We start to squirm, make weird noises, or come up with any random thing we can to break the silence.

Our fear of silence makes sense since nothingness is not considered a valuable goal in life. Imagine saying to your parents, "Mom and Dad, I know you said you wanted me to be a lawyer, but I have decided to be nothing. See ya!" I don't think Mom would be proud of your new goal.

I mean the following very literally: nothing is the greatest achievement anyone, including Jesus, Buddha, the president, Johnny Depp, Captain Jack Sparrow, or you could ever hope to attain. Unfortunately, nobody has ever attained it, but that is beside the point.

As an adult, I was afraid of losing myself in the silence because I thought I would become a "stupid nothing" (not that I was incredibly smart to begin with, which was to my advantage, I suppose). My teacher had told me that I had come to this earth to get stupid. I laughed, but he was right. Getting stupid was the best thing I could do.

Often, what many perceive as intelligent is really stupid and vice versa. In the way of nothing, these examples of stupidity masquerading as intelligence become a never-ending source of bliss and enjoyment. The world is a comedy. Watch it, and you will laugh your ass off.

Speaking of laughing, the DVD called *Rediscovering Life* by Anthony de Mello is one of my teacher's favourites. In it, de

Mello summarised what it means to live like a king. He said that essentially it means knowing no anxieties or tensions of any kind, leaving you with only undiluted happiness. When people asked him what he did to be happy, he replied that he didn't actually do anything to be happy because you can't acquire happiness. Why? Because you already have it! In our stupidity, we spend our whole time blocking happiness, but if we stop blocking it, we'll have it!

When Nothing Inspires You

When nothing inspires you, be inspired by nothing. This is the way of nothing.

There is a limit to the number of books you can read, DVDs you can watch, or teachers you can listen to in order to get your fix on consciousness. That may work for a few years, but eventually it is not enough, at least not for permanent inspiration. Eventually, you have to face nothingness alone and be inspired by it, especially when you don't have a sage to listen to, like when you are at work. Maybe your boss is all you have and your only inspiration. (Scary, eh?).

When nothing is in the way, we take inspiration from our favourite sources not because we want to take in something we don't have, but to share in the resonance. When those sources are not available, it is an opportunity to see inspiration in everything, especially in those people or things you don't want to see it in! My teacher used to say that those "special people" are our angels because they give us an opportunity to let go.

I still love to listen to spiritual teachers and read books about non-duality because they remind me of what is important. Never underestimate the potential to forget that it is all about the stillness. Keep it fresh and alive.

Living the way of nothing gives you the constant joy of self-exploration that relies on nothing external. You literally have all you need. When you get inspiration out of the thin air of nothing, then like magic nothing is in the way of freedom. Now you pick up the book or listen to the teacher, and they resonate with the total freedom of the nothingness you are living in by your own authority and as one of the divine sages of the way of nothing. Nobody can take that away because there is nobody.

All inspiration is rooted in the unbounded creativity of all that is. It comes from nowhere and looks like nothing in particular. If we have the capacity of attention and alertness, we often see that the source is the unlikeliest people or things. This apparent contradiction is the magic of nothingness playing with you.

Imagine that the guy who is so annoying that nobody can stand to be around him, and who you pray every day not to work with, is suddenly face-to-face with you. Inside your head you are screaming, "No!" When you make this situation about you, you can miss the gift. Grace doesn't always come in a sweet and gentle way. It can take any form on the inside or outside. It comes to show you where your attention is and to give an opportunity to be empty again. Being nothing means being the infinite capacity or the faceless face for the hidden inspiration.

It is true that the greatest leaps of awakening come out of nowhere. You would imagine that listening to non-dual talks or reading a certain book could do it, which is true, but they also set a limit on the infinite. There are no rules or limits. Freedom does not look like anything, and is fully open to all life has to offer even when it looks like shit. The shit turns into "holy shit!"

This is Shiva and Shakti playing together, Christ and the Holy Spirit, and the nothingness and everything-ness. They swallow each other up in their infinite love, leaving only oneness. They are inseparable as *satchitananda*. This is inspiration!

Nothing but Eternity

Eternity seems like a long time from the perspective of this one sliver in time we have called now. It goes backwards and forwards forever, but you get just this piece of it. (God can be a little cheap sometimes). The you-centre is always moving in and out of time just like a time traveller but without all the fun benefits of seeing the past and the future like in the movies.

When there is awareness of nothingness, a door opens. This frees you from being wrapped up in this little present moment, which is just a starting point for an unlimited moment. This moment now takes on a whole new freshness, becoming a completely impersonal, eternal moment that swallows up your time travelling, leaving nothing but eternity.

Like the nothingness itself, eternity has largely been unexplored. If you are unaware of this nothingness, the eternal nature seems hidden. This is obvious when you consider that you create time by thinking in time. Thinking can only happen in time. By thinking, you support the idea that you are limited to your body in space and time. Thinking reinforces your identity, which in turn is supported by your thinking. Does this habit sound familiar? You come from the past and have your future to work on. This time travelling is highly addictive because it's entertaining. The mind loves to time travel.

Even when the you-centre that you think you are becomes more refined and is thinking less and less, you still trick yourself out of eternity. You do this by thinking you are close to freedom. In the way of nothing, there is nothing in the way and this is already eternal freedom. By being addicted to achievement, you get caught in a vicious circle.

Of course when we try to figure out this eternal moment, we dig ourselves into a hole. I remember trying very hard to identify what was me and gently trying to force it into nothingness. I would judge myself when my attention moved into the future or when I had my "enlightenment thoughts." What I didn't realise was that all of that had nothing to do with me as a separate individual. Eternity was not something I could figure out because it transcends the mind, which is only ever occurring in time.

By being actively aware (without you) in nothing at all, stillness builds. This seems to stop time, which is common in meditation practices. Many students report time going really fast or slowing down so that two minutes seems like thirty or the reverse. The interesting thing about this experience is that in all cases the students disappear into the eternal moment. They usually don't recognise it as such simply because identity re-emerges immediately after.

This does not mean that when you disappear there are no thoughts, emotions, or sensations, just that the centre of identity has disappeared. This can happen with consciousness there or without it; either way it disappears. When it happens consciously, it becomes easier to allow the process of dissolving since the reward is eternal peace, resulting in a healthy addiction.

Movements of energy are not required to stop in order to enter the eternal moment. I think that this is an important distinction. Paradoxically, the you-centre can be quietly on the sidelines, but then instantly you vanish in the absolute purity of the moment.

What happens is the great wow of the silence of nothingness. It grabs you before you can do anything, and you are out of time—literally.

The wonderful thing about nothingness is that there is no end to the discovery of eternity. It keeps going and going, and it is alive with everything. Nothingness is not reserved just for the quiet, still moments of meditation but also for the busy airport or the supermarket. It happens by accident until you give it a little attention. A little attention goes a long way to unravelling the mystery.

The states of consciousness have no sway over this eternity of nothingness. In fact, the eternal has them all within.

In theory, if you believe in a past and a future, it contains the birth and the death of this universe and an infinite number of universes. This eternal moment is the empty container that contains all your past lives and future lives in this universe, if you believe in that. The story of you has been recreated over and over in eternity for no reason at all.

You are not the stories themselves but existence as it is. Why would something eternal need a cover story for your existence? A story is reason enough.

Why do you go to the movies? To be entertained, right? Nothingness is being entertained, and in that sense you are no different from the screen or from eternity. Eternity is like that as well, being nothing actively enjoying the manifestation of every-thing.

By dissolving in eternity, we lose the mental energy to figure it out because we are in a state of awe and wonder. This is a realm of beauty that nothing can touch. We lose ourselves in favour of nothing but the enjoyment of the show. Let me tell you, the seats are way better in the eternal moment. There is nothing better than that!

No-Mind

What we call the mind is just a bunch of thoughts associated with you as your mind. We all have been told we have things floating around in our heads, but let me remind you that there is only nothingness. You don't even have a brain, let alone a mind. Okay, maybe you have a brain, but you don't own it—it's not yours. You are like the scarecrow in *The Wizard of Oz*. There is a reason why he is the happiest one in the bunch.

When you get right down to it, you have nothing. I hope by now this concept is not depressing but impressing. It is actually very exciting to discover you have no mind because it is one less thing you need to worry about. Remember this about mind over matter: "If you don't have a mind then it doesn't matter."

My teacher once told me to go looking for my mind. So I closed my eyes and went looking for it. I still have not found it. Go ahead and try to find the mind; I will wait for you.

What did you see when you looked? If your mind is similar to mine (you should be so lucky), then it is just another thought appearing out of nowhere. The mind is a concept. You could say that you have a no-mind, a container or nothingness for every-thing to happen in, including the apparent happening of you. Of course you don't have it—it has you. It has the you-centre within it as a concept. By now you should realise that you are the infinite that contains all concepts, including the concepts of me, you, and that weird one over there.

If you take apart your mind, you find nothing at all but infinite potential. If you take apart your brain you will find flesh, nerves, neurons, synapses, chemicals, and electrical impulses. The infinite energy of potential manifests as your actual brain, as well as trillions of cells and neurons, to form your unique puppet body. This is your imprint or incarnation—maybe one of a thousand? How did you do all that? Good job!

You have the same mind Jesus had, the same mind as Buddha! Only the content is different. The potential is exactly the same. There is the same potential for a star, an extraterrestrial, a cat, or a human. They are the same in all space and time. It happens from eternity without effort because no-mind is involved in the process.

While you are looking for your mind, look for yourself as well, but only if you are not taking it seriously. Some people have spent years searching for "the sense of self." But guess what is looking for it? The sense of self is the only thing that has a motive to find and destroy itself. This is a nasty habit. You are better off smoking than trying to destroy yourself!

Let's just agree that you exist, okay? But if you're still not sure, here is a quick way to find out that will save you some time. In your head, say: "Hello? Is there anybody there?" Now listen quietly. If your hear nothing, then you have your answer. Great job! If you get an answer back, then you are talking to yourself. Don't worry, you don't have to head directly to the psychiatrist; we all talk to ourselves. Most of us, however, have no idea how much we talk to ourselves. If fact, we have many versions of ourselves that talk to each other inside our heads, and this is considered normal. Is this crazy or what? No wonder people are scared to go inside themselves. I will take the silence of nothingness over the insane carnival happening inside my head any day.

What you appear to be is the content appearing in the no-mind. It is that simple. It is context versus content. Nothingness is the source of what appears as the mind or as your mind. What you are is context or no-mind.

In the way of nothing, there is nothing in the way. It is valuable to play with what does not take anything seriously at all. By exploring that, the clarity of no-mind and no-you becomes obvious, happening despite you and your sense of self. Doing anything, unless it's just for the love of exploring nothing, can be a waste of time. The path of no-path is the swiftest because it is a path of joy.

What about your brain and body, your puppet? If there is no you, then how does your puppet move around eat, drink, and be merry?

This is a very interesting subject that is worth exploring. Another little exercise is to stop doing anything and see what happens. For example, I decided that I was going to see if I was needed to make things happen in this world or if it was just nothing moving. I was lying down doing nothing but being attentive to the silence. Then I had to go pee as I sometimes do (more than most). I decided that I was not going to make the decision to go pee as a separate me. Maybe I would pee the bed — I didn't know. Eventually, I watched as I got up and went to the bathroom, and peeing happened without my individual will. I know this is fascinating, but maybe you will have a better example when you do the experiment for yourself.

There are a billion examples of things happening on their own like tying shoelaces and riding a bike. It has happened to you millions of times, but it goes on unnoticed. These little examples of no-you are a clue into the way of nothing and are worthy of exploration. The truth is: you are not there in control of your activities as much as you think you are. This is not just a concept, as you will find out through attention to nothingness.

Your sense of self only seems to be there if you think it's important. Otherwise you would constantly be repeating loud and proud, "It's *me* who's going to pee. *I* am tying *my* shoelaces. Good for *me*." Maybe you said these things as a child, but now that you know how to do them they're effortless. Who cares anymore? They're not your greatest achievements. The sense of self is not needed for mundane activities, which are automatic by-products of programming and conditioning. We still take credit for them, however.

It is easier to see the lack of you in simple activities, which is why I'm starting there. As a child I would sometimes wonder what my life would be like if I'd been born in another body. I felt so lucky to have been born in Calgary, Alberta. To me it was the greatest city in the world. It wasn't until I left that I started to really see how diverse the world stage is. The possibilities for programming and conditioning the human brain and body are almost endless.

The human brain starts out as an innocent and fresh sponge ready to soak everything up. The influence of genetics and your mother's womb were at play before birth. Hopefully, she was chanting the Vedas and eating carrots or you are screwed. Then you were exposed to the environment: where in the world you happened to be and the personality of your parents, relatives, and everyone else. There was also school, society, culture, religion, TV, and idols. For fun, let's also throw in other notions like astrology, karma, and past lives. I have to stop because I am starting to feel bad for you. I am not sure how you even made it to this point in the book, but I guess miracles do happen. So many factors contributed to your story that it boggles the mind.

All these factors can lead to compassion for your mother or for any soul on earth. With all these influences on us, no wonder we do the stupid things we do over and over again. Who's to blame? It's everybody's and nobody's fault. I guess they cancel each other out, leaving us nothing again. It always comes back to nothing.

What does this all have to do with you? Nothing.

What have you contributed to your condition? Nothing.

When you see from a fresh and innocent perspective, it is no accident that you do what you do and act like you act. You are nothing more than a puppet, and your brain has been programmed just like a computer. It's a bit like in the movie *The Matrix*.

I like to look at it backwards. Instead of considering the source of our brain and body activity, let's take away the source.

What allows for the programming of the brain and the movement of the body? It is the empty sponge of awareness, which is a quality of nothingness.

If we remove that awareness from all of us by lifting it out of the tops of our heads, we shut down, and the puppet goes limp. Now your body and brain are gone from your attention. Take a rest here for a moment. Enjoy the freedom from you and your programming. Your puppet awaits further instructions from the infinite.

Programming is not bad, and you are not bad, even with all your special and weird characteristics. They are what make the collective and individual stories unique, and you could not do without your particular one. Nothingness programmed you, just for shits and giggles. We are comedy for each other.

Whenever you are ready, you can let the awareness that is in your control drop back into your head to reactivate yourself again. Or maybe you want to stay deactivated for a while to explore the no-mind without any distractions.

Keep Moving—Nothing to See Here

On the path of no-path are many signs that tempt us to pull over and stop. Sometimes bright neon signs attract our attention with their clever advertising. Sometimes the signs are more subtle, but each one is designed to get us to pull over and stop.

Signs can take the form of an idea that will help you get where you are going. This includes any ideas mentioned here. The mind loves to help you get to your special enlightenment. It is always seeking the ultimate answer so it can say, "Aha, I get it!" An aha is wonderful, but it's only a sign along the road pointing the way.

Instead of going anywhere, we get stuck on the side of the road staring at the sign. Sometimes we get so blinded by our ideas that we wander around the road until hopefully we get the idea that getting hit by a truck will turn us into roadkill. But instead of having the attitude, "Keep moving—nothing to see here," we just go out and grab another idea. For most of us, years go by before we are willing to hold nothing and walk straight ahead into the unknown. Ironically, holding nothing happens naturally anyway; only an idea makes it look difficult. The natural way of being is to hold nothing.

Looking back into the past is like clinging to roadkill and praying it will be resurrected. Leave the raccoon on the side of the road—it is dangerous. Raccoon zombies are the worst kind!

The worst-case scenario is that we believe in our idea so strongly that we refuse to move. This really only makes a difference to the one who seems to be stuck.

Virtually everyone has a big bright sign on their head saying, "I am so and so." It can take courage to be naked without anything to point at or claim. After all, what are you if you're not pointing at an idea?

Even the idea that you are nothingness is just another sign

along the road. Even facts are just ideas when it comes to what is reality. For example, I could say, "I am short." But I don't walk around thinking, "I am short!" Someone has to point it out by saying it. Then I notice it and say, "That's funny because I thought I was taller. Look at me—I'm so short." Being short is not something I need to hold onto, nor is any idea.

The tricky part is when we have subtler ideas about what we are. We have read the books and meditated, so now we know that we are infinite and enlightened. But do we go around thinking, "I am infinite, I am nothingness," over and over again? Wouldn't that be crazy? That would be a mantra or an affirmation at best.

Anything we identify with has the potential to appear real if we believe it, and nothing becomes a story again. Our human nature is to keep following the signs, never quite getting to the destination. Of course, in the way of nothing, we are already at the destination right now. There is nothing in the way of this. These words you are reading are just signs like anything else; there is no truth in them. The truth is beyond an idea—it is nothingness without the idea of nothingness. Nothingness is what is being pointed to. This is the awesomeness of already being free!

Every thought and emotion comes from out of the stillness like a fish jumping out of water. There is no need to analyse the fish. Yet when we notice ourselves grabbing it, it is so easy to let it go. It takes effort to hold onto a slippery, slimy fish all day. It is much easier to say, "Keep moving—nothing to see here." Let the fish carry on happily swimming and jumping because that is what it does naturally. Thoughts and emotions are energy in motion. They love to keep moving around because that is their job. This is the function of energy—to move. Our thoughts and emotions are rivers moving into the ocean. They are not meant to be manipulated or controlled. Why would you want to do that anyway?

When we start to notice how easy it is to let things be what they are, we discover that it is actually easier to stay with nothingness than to hold onto a passing sign. Eventually, meditation becomes effortless because stopping to think takes tremendous energy. Usually, we think it's the opposite—that waking up is hard and thinking is easy, but only because of our habit of ignorance. We are constantly using up energy avoiding the simplicity of nothingness. We habitually use energy to avoid what we are.

The content of the mind seems important because there is insufficient contrast between the peace that comes from silence and the quacking ducks in our head. As we taste complete silence, the quacking remains but seems less attractive than the pond of stillness.

When we allow what naturally moves to move and what is still to be still, they simply become one. The problem is just the illusion of control by the separate identity, which is just a natural part of life that comes and goes like the slimy fish.

Keep moving—nothing to see here.

Nobody There to Care

With nothing in the way, there is nobody to care. You are more like air than you may realise. Does air care?

In some ways, air is analogous to the way of nothing. It is always around, filling up space. We breathe it all day, and yet for the most part it is not in our awareness. But hold your breath for a while, and it becomes the most precious thing in the world. In the same way that air is precious, so is the way of nothing. But it goes unnoticed because it is the background of everything. Likewise, we don't see air; we see through it or breathe it. We don't need a separate identity to breathe; nor do we need it to live life. It just seems that way out of habit.

Like the easiness of breathing air, the easiness of nothing makes it crazy to be a special somebody. When there is a special somebody, you have all the problems that go along with that process of identifying. This means taking your life personally and being responsible for fulfilling a whole list of conditions related to your survival and what you need in order to be happy. Now the air starts to get heavy, and maybe you are having a little trouble breathing under this weight.

Sometimes it is a good thing to identify or re-identify with being a somebody because it is a good reminder of everything, that doing so entails. By putting your hand in the fire enough times, you can learn that it hurts, and you can stop it anytime. You'll keep putting your hand back in the fire, but don't take that seriously—just laugh at it.

When you are not there, life has a wonderfully spontaneous way of taking care of itself. Nothingness is not a stupid nothing, but it is the source of stupidity. Thank God it is also the source of intelligence. You do not have to be intelligent, wise, or responsible because in the way of nothing, there is nobody there to care.

You can save for retirement because the bank automatically

takes money out of your account whenever you want it to. For just five minutes of your time, you never have to worry about getting old and having no money—God took care of it. Do you really need to be there to make sure you will have money in the future? What other problems do you have? All problems in life can be solved with technology, Google, and without your being there to care.

Your bills get paid as long as you get up to go to work. You eat because you get hungry, and you get angry at your co-worker when it's appropriate, but all of that is nothing moving and happening. Life is easy without you and all your problems. Tell them to a special somebody who cares.

Nothingness Is Sacredness

Nothing is sacred because is it divine. It is lucky for someone to lose their specialness in the divine. Even seeking the divine is a rare thing in the world. When you discover it, it is appropriate to make it a sacred experience for yourself. This does not mean lighting incense and chanting to the gods necessarily unless you happen to find that sacred. If sacred to you is eating chocolate, then that is the experience of divine sacredness because you disappear in the love of chocolate. Sacredness may be a walk with your son, getting ice cream, or watching your favourite movie. The sacred is all around you!

Quieting the chaos of the world in order to honour the sacredness of that space is indeed beautiful. The infinite also tends to make itself more available to those that appreciate it. Nothingness is a little bit Self-absorbed.

When you love someone, you put time and energy into the relationship. This is not something you have to do but something you love to do. This applies to your big Self as well. Putting time and energy into it is like falling in Love. By falling in love with the sacredness of nothing, you fall in love with everything. Suddenly everything becomes sacred. Everything is sacred because it is all yourself.

This is oneness whereby the self has no other. Divinity is that shining one in all.

Sacredness does not mean that we take a position of respect because we are told something deserves our respect. Laughing at a funeral can honour the sacred space of the dead as much or more so than reading from the Bible. Sacredness has no form, for it is unlimited. Every step on earth is sacred; we only need to have eyes to see it.

Sacredness is a natural by-product of nothingness. Once we are bitten by the nothingness bug, every step we take turns into a miracle of wonder. Now every event is amazing. Even blinking our eyes is a big deal. No words can begin to describe the aliveness of that sacred nothingness. It is like a child walking for the first time. We are like babies on the verge of the incredible wonder of discovery.

All of creation is praising the aliveness of this. In the silence of that space, the heart sings a song of constant joy that brings tears to the angels of nothingness.

When you are willing to give sacredness a little bit of attention, it will grab you and love you to death—literally. It is like the saying, "Take one step towards me and I will take a thousand towards you."

This is the Divine Mother.

If Nothingness Could Speak, What Would It Say?

Nothing would say what you say and do what you do! *There is nothing in the way!* This is the mystery of no-you.

There is only freedom and the seeing and not seeing happening within that freedom. Liberation and bondage are only concepts floating around. Who needs to be free when there is nobody at all? Who is there to care if you are free? Your life and where you are right now as you read these words is perfect. There is nothing you could do to be more conscious than you are now.

I can hear someone saying, "But of course I could be more conscious!" That is a fantasy, an ideal that you will never reach. Even if you could reach that ideal, you would have another pretend somebody in your head, somebody you imagine would be more conscious in the future.

Having ideals is the opposite of being conscious, by the way. Being conscious is seeing to the core that nothing is missing now. It is the disappearance of ideals. Life is never ideal! There will always be something missing as long as you are a somebody looking for something. The seeker scene is endless.

This seeking is the perfect way to avoid love. Love cannot devour you as long as you are not okay with what is. Love is seeing yourself as you are, not as you should be. Love is nothing allowing everything. This accepts you and your story; which is the content to love's context. Love is the context of what appears to move and change. Wisdom sees the way of nothing in which there is only love. You are the context of love. Love is exploring the mystery of no-you.

What can you do? May I suggest a path of joy?

This is the way of nothing—the path of joy and nothing in the way.

There is nothing else to say.

Bibliography

Blofeld, John. *The Zen Teaching of Huang Po*. Grove Press, 1958.

de Mello, Anthony. *Rediscovering Life*, DVD. DeMello Stroud Spirituality Center. Church of the Epiphany.

"The Pitch," *Seinfeld*, 43rd episode, 1992. Written by Larry David produced by Tom Cherones

Visit Paramananda at:
www.paramanandaishaya.com

To learn about the Practice of the Bright Path visit:
www.thebrightpath.com

MANTRA
BOOKS

We publish books on Eastern religions and philosophies.
Books that aim to inform and explore the various
traditions, that began rooted in East and
have migrated West.